HOW TO RIDE AND JUMP YOUR BEST

HOW TO RIDE AND JUMP YOUR BEST

by Barbara Van Tuyl

GROSSET & DUNLAP
A National General Company
Publishers
New York

Fondly dedicated to Lisa Longo and Fancy

Contents

HOW TO
RIDE AND JUMP
YOUR BEST

Introduction

The first complete written record of horsemanship that has come down to us is that of the Greek general Xenophon, dating back some four hundred years before Christ. Both Western and English schools of horsemanship point to Xenophon as the father of their respective styles. Since both can find examples to substantiate their claims, it appears that Xenophon did produce a common denominator for all types of riding. With the passage of time, riding branched out and became more stylized.

In all fairness to the earliest riders, riding was simply part of the great network of survival. Suddenly transformed into superior beings able to dominate their foot-bound brothers as well as their environment, those first mounted beings were supermen. They could hunt better, fight longer, and retreat faster than their unmounted competitors. In those times even daily survival was a test many failed. Once mastery over the horse had been accomplished, no man could imagine life without the horse as his means of transportation, beast of burden, charger in war, and integral part of day-to-day living. So it was, until farming and transportation became mechanized and riding became mainly a pastime for sport and pleasure.

1

The riding of today has come a long way from the time of the Spanish Conquistadores, who fathered the Western style of riding, and the early New England and Virginia settlers, who brought the English style of horsemanship to the New World. Since the horse is no longer part of a way of life, those interested in pursuing the art of riding must seek competent instruction when available and convenient.

An important part of learning to ride is *reading,* but this is often ignored. As William C. Steinkraus points out most clearly in *Riding and Jumping:*

because of the oft-repeated remark that 'you can't learn to ride by reading a book about it'. . .that you can only learn, in a sort of intuitive way, by doing, and that reading or even thinking seriously about riding is rather pointless, too many young riders are doomed to groping too long in a forest of problems solved long ago. . .I can recall my astonishment. . .at finding, in books written two or three centuries ago, minute descriptions of 'discoveries' that I had made for myself only after a long period of trial and error.

Such commentary by one of today's leading riders and dedicated students of equitation leads one to wonder why riders are so reluctant to spend some time reading about the techniques of their sport.

I think that the answer lies in the fact that it is extremely difficult to communicate a mental picture of a physical action. A whole spider web of misinformation and misconception could come from this tricky area of communication.

For example let us say that a beginning rider decided to further his knowledge by reading a well-known book on horsemanship. If any mix-up should occur in the translation of the written word to the mental image there is no immediate way to clarify the thought. Rarely is an alternative phrasing or method presented which might at least suggest that there is more than one way to ride a horse.

Bearing this in mind it is interesting to note that there is a wide range of diversification within English riding, with the hunter/jumper seat claiming the most internal disagreement. Over long periods of time, even old pros in this particular field are never consistent in their thinking.

Pressured by alert newcomers, more difficult courses, a greater demand for better-grade, more highly schooled horses, and the ever present image of the United States Prix de Nations team, instructors and professionals across the country are being forced into experimenting with and questioning the old schools while attempting to create more useful and enduring new schools. Those experts who fail to recognize the current trend toward Olympic-type courses in the jumper divisions and hunter courses are swiftly falling out of favor.

Take, for example, a once-successful professional instructor who refuses to accept the difference between riding twice around the outside edge of a ring over four rail fences spaced evenly apart, and riding all over a ring to fences set at every possible angle and spaced unevenly. Phrases such as "from the short corner," "riding a line," and a "steady two to a long one" are not a part of this man's vocabulary. Today's courses demand familiarity with such concepts. If they are not expressed in exactly the same way, so much the better. As long as the meaning is clear, the instruction is effective. Instead, this person is living in the Dark Ages as far as competitive riding is concerned. His pupils, ill-equipped with a meaningless "get him in your hand," are as well-prepared to meet the challenges at a horse show as Sir Lancelot would be if he arrived mounted and in full armor at Broadway and 42nd Street during the rush hour.

Fortunately for the equestrian community as a whole, the controversy over today's hunter and jumper courses does not end simply with how they are to be ridden. There exists almost as much disagreement as to the type of horse required to satisfactorily negotiate an Olympic-type course as about his schooling and that of his rider. The Germans, English, Irish, and Italians seem to favor a heavier breed all around (perhaps seven-eighths to three-quarters bred). The South Americans prefer nimble, smaller types, and North Americans the popular American Thoroughbred.

The different preferences and controversies between people and nations have had beneficial effects. As the courses improve, the horses rise to the challenge. The rules under which jumping competitions are judged are designed to select the best all-around horses. Judgments are based on which can jump the most diversified obstacles at the greatest height from the most difficult approaches in the shortest time without incurring faults. Hunter courses, on the other hand, while less difficult from the standpoint of unusual jumps, time element, or varying heights, are also challenging. Striving for eight equal fences makes considerable demands on both horse and rider.

The Horse

Just how much can one ask of a horse? What does he do instinctively? What must he be taught? How does a rider request and accept the responses he wants? Under what circumstances should the horse be punished and how? What should the horse be praised for and what form should praise take?

Questions like these often deluge the mind of a beginning rider. Since all too often he is not really familiar with horses there is little he can do to solve his dilemma. Let us, therefore, take a closer look at this animal.

The horse is basically a dumb animal. He ranks low on the intelligence scale, and there are any number of professional horsemen who would gladly place him at the very bottom of the list. He frightens easily and is in fact a very timid beast. As a rule he is not aggressive although the amount of spunk varies with each individual, occasionally producing a true outlaw or rogue. His athletic ability is not outstanding simply because he is a horse, nor need he display any particular talent or inclination just because of a certain lineage.

His mind is a simple one. He learns best through simple repetition—practice without mishap. Frequently this requires a large

5

amount of patience on the part of the rider. Every now and again a real whiz streaks across the path of a rider, learning everything on the first try and becoming an old hand on the second. However, horses with such steel-trap minds are indeed rare.

Fear plays a major role in the life of every horse. His otherwise faulty memory seems to record each disquieting incident with unerring accuracy. It is this overwhelming fearfulness that causes a nice horse to bolt and run for miles, a stalwart jumper to balk at a previously difficult fence, and Susie's "foolproof" pony to suddenly rear and wheel at the sight of brother Jim calmly approaching in a waving, trailing bedsheet.

Poor vision accounts for some of the horse's problems, and it takes far more courage for a horse to face up to something he finds awesome than for another creature with better vision. Not too much information is known about the visual perception of the horse, but it has been fairly well established that he does not focus well on objects closer than three or four feet. He must, therefore, rely on what he sees during his approach rather than what he sees upon his arrival. In view of this handicap, it is amazing that horses jump fences at all, much less those over seven feet high. Furthermore, there is some evidence that speed affects a horse's vision. If true, this could explain why some race horses never make the far turn and run right through the rail, or how Mary's horse could panic while going cross country and run into a telephone pole. Such incidents are not proofs of the animal's stupidity, but rather possible examples of a kind of mechanical failure in his physical structure.

The horse's powers of reason are sadly limited and unfortunately seem not to be influenced by pain or injury. For example, a horse will rush blindly back into a burning building looking for the "safety" of his own stall. Knowing this, can one honestly expect a horse to attempt a formidable jump or even to tread on suspicious-looking ground just because the rider smacks him once or twice with a crop? Not at all. Unless the horse has been taught to understand that he is being punished for disregarding the wishes of his rider, he will fail to realize that the blow from the whip is in any way connected with his reluctance to go forward. It is equally difficult for a horse to comprehend the reality of reward. The burden is on the rider, as always, to make his meanings quite clear. Reward is often the absence of punishment, but to be recognized as such the absence must be *total*. It does no good at all to lavishly praise and pat your horse for a job well done if the hand still hold-ing the reins remains inflexible so that he is being rapped in the gums as he naturally bobs his head while walking.

The horse is indeed a complex animal, running the gamut of temperament fromextraordinary docility to occasional roguishness. He is capable of extreme generosity and courage as well as displays of unusual athletic heroics. His destiny or self-determination, as it were, is literally in the hands of his riders. It is this endless variety of dispositions that piques the interest and challenges the skill of every enthusiastic rider and ultimately lures him into becoming a diehard participant in the sport.

Strange though it may seem, riders for the most part tend to *underestimate* the competence of their horses. Despite proof to the contrary demonstrated by the top-notch performers of higher levels of dressage, the words "But my horse (or I) can't do that!" are heard all too frequently throughout the horse world.

Much of this hesitation stems from the rider's insecurity. Cer-tainly he should not tax either himself or his horse with impossible situations, but he should familiarize himself with the horse's po-tential.

To this end a rider needs only to watch a well-executed Grand Prix dressage test, most notably in the areas of collection and ex-tension as well as the movements of lateral tracking. The backlash-type pivots and the spins and lightning sprints of a World Cham-pionship cutting horse or a Lippizaner on exhibition give a pretty fair idea of just what a horse is capable of doing.

After viewing a number of diversified exhibitions and competi-tions one will quickly realize that the horse has a variety of for-ward speeds. They begin in a flat-footed walk and progress to a slow, ordinary, and extended trot, then increase to a slow, ordinary, and extended canter, and climax in a gallop. All these gaits involve the rhythmic sequential presentation of the horse's feet. It is the act of first *attaining* and then *maintaining* a specified gait and cadence at any speed that provides a goal or yardstick for measur-ing one's progress.

When compared to that of a dog or cat, the horse's jumping ability is hampered by his shortened spine. Nonetheless, he has done well despite his limitations and has jumped heights in excess of seven feet. The world's high-jumping mark is eight feet three inches, achieved by the great Heatherbloom.

An open jumper negotiating a triple-bar type of spread fence.

An open jumper negotiating a vertical fence and beginning to turn in midflight.

A hunter demonstrating superb form over a rail fence.

Of course not too many riders wish to ride down to such formidable obstacles, but the fences at an average horse show range from three and one-half to four feet in the hunter division, and anywhere from three feet, nine inches to six feet or more in the jumper division.

Good-quality cutting horses are extraordinarily nimble. At times they seem to move faster than the eye can follow, and certainly faster than a steer can move. There would seem to be little basis for comparison between the cutting horse and the jumper, but the turns, springs, and agility demonstrated so ably by the former are readily applicable to the time turns and short-cut courses negotiated by the latter.

The extreme muscle control and suppleness shown by Lippizaners or horses engaged in dressage are considerably greater than required for less exacting endeavors. Muscle control and suppleness indicate the type of performance a horse may achieve. Elementary dressage (which actually means "schooling") provides a sound basis for most hunters and jumpers. Much like human setting-up exercises, dressage builds suppleness and muscle tone. Simple moves like leg-yielding, serpentines, flying changes, and turns on the forehand or haunches are fair game for any horse and within the ability of the average accomplished rider.

Without expending any more effort than going to a few shows or exhibitions, one may discover that Equus has a long list of talents and accomplishments. He can move forward in any number of speeds either with utter abandon or under complete control. He may lift his feet high off the ground and place them, or skim the ground with his hoofs barely touching. He can spin right and left in the wink of an eye, or change direction midstride by the mere shifting of weight. He can halt, back, or stand motionless from just about any position. His head may be carried high or low, nose in or out. He may jump high, wide, and handsome, as it were, demonstrating manners and form or derring-do against a clock.

Not every horse can do any or all of these things, of course, but the scope of their accomplishment exists, undeniably.

Since the horse lacks the ability to reason, he compensates by acting on instinct. He cannot think out a logical reason why thunder and lightning, marshy ground, or streams should be regarded with a healthy respect. Yet intuitively he *knows* that these things bear watching; it would be an unusually bold animal that would let them pass unnoticed. The horse also does other things by instinct. For instance he can feel the dip and swell of the ground and adjust his stride to get the best and smoothest foothold. Left to his own devices he will switch his leads to accommodate the slightest change of direction. Inasmuch as nature has already provided the horse with the fundamentals, these tendencies need only to be strengthened and developed by the rider.

If the horse were still living as a wild creature and were not engaged in many activities for man's use and recreation, it would not be necessary to teach him anything. Living free, the horse is perfectly well equipped to fend for himself. However, the years of domestication have taken much of the resourcefulness away from him, and he has become increasingly dependent on man. In addition to this forced dependence, man's transformation of the horse from a working animal to a source of sport and pleasure has placed a whole new category of demands on him. As an extension of his natural self-protectiveness, he is expected to run like the wind for the sport of Thoroughbred racing; he is asked to negotiate a nightmare of obstacles in steeplechase, and he must learn to collect and extend his natural gaits in a sort of horse's ballet for dressage. In the process of learning to do all these things, he must be taught to use his natural endowments to the best possible advantage. Elasticity of body and gait are of paramount importance for any of the more involved maneuvers as well as all jumps. The lessons in bending, flexing, and extending must be thoroughly learned before proceeding to the next level.

The purpose of the rider's being astride the animal at all is to transmit his ideas and desires to the horse for action. To this end he has a number of tools at his disposal. He may speak to the horse through his hands, legs, seat, voice, or any combination thereof. He may speak loudly or whisper, so long as his intentions are clear to the animal. His signals must be well defined, and he must ask the horse to do only those things that the animal has already mastered. Exercises or movements that are still in the learning phases must be treated as just that and approached on a step-by-step basis.

Since he tends to confuse easily, a defined command must be clear to the horse at all times. If, for example, a rider wishes to circle to the right but has forgotten to ease off or to release his left rein, he can hardly expect the horse to turn when he is being given the signal to stop. Nor can he repeatedly halt an eager horse in front of the same fence and then expect the horse to jump over it.

Under no circumstances should a horse be punished for a simple display of high spirits—that is, a short-lived, all-in-fun kind of leaping around indulged in by some animals when they are exuberant. If a horse cuts up in this manner and then settles down to business he should not be penalized. His mouth should not be pulled and yanked nor should his hindparts be smacked with a crop. If a rider anticipates a rougher ride than he wishes to sit on at the time, the animal should be longed or turned out prior to being ridden to avoid a confrontation.

Punishment should not be meted out for stopping at a strange fence or for a reluctance to cross into unfamiliar territory. The animal should be allowed to investigate what is frightening him, and several attempts should be made to gain his confidence before resorting to the stronger urging of bat or spurs.

The horse who does not bend his body properly or pick up his leads precisely (or in some instances at all), whose pace is erratic, or whose jumping definitely must be improved does not necessarily need discipline. Instead, the rider must use all his resources to produce the desired result. Only after establishing beyond any doubt that the animal is stubbornly resisting should the bat, spurs, or hands be strongly applied. It is important, however, to remember that at such a time, having determined the necessity for such measures, discipline must be swift and firm. A light tap with the whip or spurs will do little and more likely than not will serve only to aggravate the horse.

Rough use of the hands, a driving seat, strong use of the leg—with or without spurs—and a bat are the most common punishment devices. Other training aids such as draw lines, side reins, or martingales may be implemented as disciplinary steps.

Assuming that the horse is given a proper signal and that he either answers adequately or attempts to do the right thing, what then? Either result is praiseworthy, because the horse made an effort to obey. It may be the poorest excuse for a figure eight that has ever been witnessed by man, but if the horse seemed willing to make the necessary circles and did his best to go where he was told, his efforts must be duly noted and rewarded. Once the intent is present, it is only a matter of time and practice before the most awkward components become a pleasing whole.

Seat

In order to discuss some of the problems and techniques that are an integral part of hunter-seat riding and jumping, we must first realize that we are dealing with two very different and frequently unpredictable entities—a *horse* and a *rider*. Then, having established in our own minds the individuality of each horse and each rider, we are forced into the immediate realization that since such a wide range of variables can affect the rapport between just one horse and his usual rider, there cannot possibly be clear-cut formulas that are guaranteed to work with every horse or every rider.

Recognizing that there is no single correct method is a giant step toward furthering your general riding knowledge. It opens the way, furthermore, for you to gather and accept as much information on a given subject as might be available. One of the most often-repeated opening phrases between fellow horsemen whenever they get together is "Have you ever had a horse that. . .?" After which, the speaker goes on to describe a particular horse that has presented him with an unusual problem, or at least one with which he has not had any previous experience. Regardless of whether the person's problem is relatively common or is indeed unique, there is always someone who will answer, "Have you tried. . .?" or "That's the kind of thing Susie's horse used to do and she changed the bit

14

from a. . ." and then go on to relate all his experiences that might apply to the case presented. Rarely will a horseman laugh at or lightly dismiss another horseman's difficulties with *any* horse, because he knows that tomorrow he may be having similar problems with one of his own equines. He can save himself a good deal of time and effort just by finding out what another person has tried and what the results have been.

This type of discussion is equally commonplace among riding instructors, particularly when comparing the more stylized equitation techniques with which a good instructor "stamps" his students, or when attempting to adapt these methods to a particular pupil's needs or physical limitations. For example, should the topic of conversation be the carriage of the rider's foot in the stirrup, you will probably find as many opinions of what is an acceptable position as there are persons present. While they might all agree that the stirrup is carried on the ball of the foot, there will most assuredly be differences of opinions as to whether it ought to be placed on the inside or the outside of the foot, how far the heel ought to be flexed, whether the toe should point in, out, or anywhere in particular, and which of the details are important and which are simply tinsel. Once an instructor or rider has arrived at what he considers the ideal position in his own mind, he must then determine how best to achieve it while taking into consideration his own body structure or that of the persons he is teaching.

Applying the ideal is much easier said than done. A person can neither be asked to ride in a way that goes against his natural body position, nor can he be asked to flex, bend, or straighten a part of himself that cannot physically be made to do so. There is no profit, furthermore, in a posture that is pleasing to the eye yet completely nonfunctional. The position for you is one that is as close to the ideal as possible but makes allowance for your own physical structure and permits your body to function at its best. As we begin to explore some of the fundamentals of hunter-seat riding and jumping, remember that each thought or principle that we examine is but one of many ways to accomplish the end result— a smooth, well-defined performance on the part of both horse and rider.

While I hasten to point out that there is no one right way of doing most things, I am equally swift to add that there are many wrong ones. For instance, you may wish to make a simple circle to the left. In order to accomplish such a move you have a number of alternatives, including using either a direct or a leading rein or various combinations of your hands, legs, and seat—depending upon how your horse has been schooled and the methods with which you are familiar. However, should you decide to cross your right hand over the horse's withers toward the left, the reins would pull upon the right side of his mouth, which can at no time be construed as a signal meaning to turn left; you would not, therefore, get the corresponding circle to the left that you mistakenly thought you had asked for.

To expand this thought further for a moment, it stands to reason that some things in hunter-seat riding are sufficiently successful that they have become the accepted way—to do, sit, or look. In most instances these are the things that are almost always likely to produce the greatest amount of control. In referring to the judging of hunter-seat equitation, the American Horse Shows Association states, "Rider should have a workmanlike appearance, seat and hands light and supple, conveying the impression of complete control should any emergency arise." It would seem that "control" is the key word here and that a good question to ask yourself whenever you are riding would be, "Do I have the most control over my horse at this moment from this position?" If the answer is "No," look for a better way to arrange your body for the utmost efficiency. Another way to think of your position is to analyze which parts of the horse's body are influenced by which parts of your own. For example, the horse's front legs, shoulder, head, and neck are most directly affected by your hands. If you use your hands most advantageously your horse will respond properly with his forehand. Your legs govern his hindquarters so the proper use of *your* legs should produce a correct reaction with *his* hind legs. It follows that the more nearly correct your position the greater effect you are able to produce on a given area and the more control you are able to exert on the horse and his performance.

CORRECT POSITION

Just what is the "ideal" position and what should it look like? In order for a horse to perform his best, either over fences or on the flat, he must be in a position that affords him the best possible balance as well as the utmost use of his head and neck. With this in mind, the rider should attempt to stay as close to the horse's center of gravity as possible and provide the least amount of interference with the horse's natural movement.

At this time it is only fair to point out that there is a specific type of human anatomy that is more readily adaptable to effective riding than any other. The perfect riding physique is comprised of a short waist, wiry build, and long legs—which is not to say that persons of different build should not ride, but rather that those who have a good riding physique are particularly well suited to the sport. A build such as this enables a person to get down deeper into the saddle and around the horse's barrel, which at the same time makes it easier for the upper body to remain in balance with the motion of the horse. A body that is long-waisted and short-legged tends to be top heavy, which makes it much more difficult to maintain good natural balance.

One of the ways to discuss the rider's posture is by analyzing its parts. The number and names of these, however, vary greatly with the locale and school of horsemanship. Therefore, let us borrow the apportionment and titles used by George H. Morris, who is the foremost riding instructor in the United States at this time as well as being a former member of the United States Equestrian Team. Mr. Morris defines the *leg* as the portion of the body that includes the knee and below; the *base* as the seat and thighs, and the *upper body* as everything which is above the base. He also uses a fourth term, *balance,* to describe a combination of the three portions of the body working together.

The distribution of the parts of the body is basically the same no matter whose teaching you choose to follow, although there are deviations of preference. Some prefer to see the stirrup iron carried off the toe, the ball of the foot, or "home" at the heel of the boot.

Legs and Base

Since the legs and the base are indeed the foundation of the hunter-seat and are therefore less mobile than the upper body, we will deal with them first. When the horse is at the halt the rider should be well positioned in the front part of the saddle, sitting on his pelvic bones. His thighs should be flat against the saddle and the inner sides of his legs should be against the sides of the horse—

When the horse is at the halt, the rider should be well positioned in the front part of the saddle, sitting on his seat bones. His thighs should be flat against the saddle.

The inner sides of the rider's legs should be against the sides of the horse. In other words, the inner knee bone and inside of his calf should be in contact with the horse's sides.

that is, his inner knee bone and inside of his calf should be in contact with the horse's sides. The toes should fall outward at an angle in keeping with the rider's conformation. The ball of the foot should be placed on the stirrup iron (whether toward the inside or outside of the iron is optional), with the heel flexed downward and slightly behind the girth.

Upper Body

The upper body is expected to be more flexible than the leg and base, which should not change at all. In the basic position at the halt, the eyes should be up and the shoulders back, with the upper body perpendicular to the ground. This vertical posture is also the correct position when the horse is stopping from another gait or when he is backing. As the horse moves into the walk, the sitting trot, or the canter, the upper body should be slightly in front of the vertical. At the posting trot or the hand gallop the rider should be inclined slightly more forward. When working on the flat, the body should not incline any farther forward than for the posting trot position. There is one other position of the upper body, but this comes as the result of riding a certain type of horse rather than an adjustment made for gait. When riding a horse that is sulky or rough and apt to hang back or balk, the rider should position his upper body slightly behind the vertical to obtain the maximum use of his back and seat as he encourages or drives the animal forward.

Hands

A rider's hands are the most difficult part of his anatomy to discipline and control. He must learn to be at the same time firm yet soft, sympathetic yet strong, fluid yet definite, and all the while he must be sensitive to the messages the horse is sending him through the reins. Many an otherwise talented rider has been halted irrevocably in his progress due to an unduly hard or insensitive set of hands, while a number of lesser natural talents have made their way far beyond their wildest expectations all because of a "beautiful" set of hands or an innately good touch with the reins.

It is virtually impossible to haul or pull a horse around a ring or a course of fences just by tugging, yanking, or snatching on the

In the basic position at the halt, the eyes should be up and the shoulders back with the upper body perpendicular to the ground, or "vertical."

As the horse moves into the walk, the sitting trot, or the canter, the upper body should be slightly in front of the vertical. Here, at the sitting trot, the rider is correctly positioned with her upper body barely in front of the vertical.

At the posting trot, the rider should be inclined slightly more forward. At no time when working on the flat should there be a forward inclination of the body any farther than in the posting trot.

Here the rider has positioned her upper body slightly behind the vertical to obtain the maximum use of her back and seat as she encourages her horse to move forward "in front of her leg."

reins. Furthermore, you cannot begin to see any results with your hands until you are willing to compromise with the horse as the situation demands. A great deal of correctness in the position of the hands depends upon the natural head carriage of the horse you are riding. However, the basic position is one in which the hands are carried over and in front of the horse's withers, fingers closed upon the reins with the thumbs on top and the palms facing each other. The hands should be slightly separated and for the most part should create a straight line from the horse's mouth to the rider's elbow. Although such a line is not always the natural one, it should not be broken by the rider's wrist turning in or out or the palms turning upward and outward. In cases where the horse's head carriage prevents the straight line, it is usually acceptable to have the line broken *above* the horse's mouth and generally improper to break it below (as would be the case if the rider lowered his hands toward his own knees or the horse's shoulder).

Elbows

In all instances the rider's elbows should be "in" — that is, close enough to his sides so that they do not flap, but not so tight or rigid that it looks as though they were permanently affixed to the rib cage.

Eyes

Although not a part of the rider's position as such, eyes play an extremely important part in the overall picture as well as in the performance of a rider both on the flat and over fences. In the show ring a rider who is constantly looking down often gives the appearance of being round-shouldered or, worse yet, *ashamed* of being there and apologetic for taking the judge's time to look at him. In the hunt field or in cross-country riding, the rider must look around and ahead to note the position of other riders as well as the lay of the land; looking down would create a definite hazard. Regardless of whether you are actively competing, practicing, or just riding for pleasure at home, you must learn to use your head and eyes to direct the rest of your body. This means that you must not only *look* where you are going, but that you must train

The basic hand position places the hands over and in front of the horse's withers, fingers closed upon the reins, with the thumbs on top and the palms facing each other.

The basic hand position with a snaffle bridle.

For the most part, the hands should create a straight line from the horse's mouth to the rider's elbow.

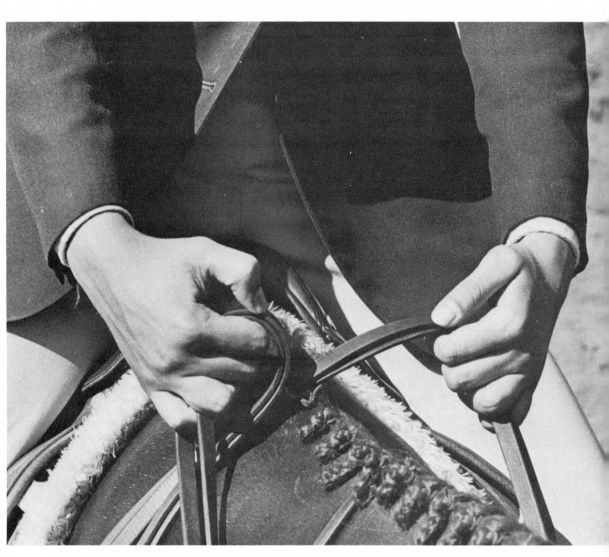

*The rider's wrists should not turn in and thus break the line
from the horse's mouth to the rider's elbow.*

Nor should they break to the outside with the palms inclined upward or outward.

In all instances the rider's elbows should be "in." They should be close enough to his sides so that they do not flap, but not so tight or rigid that they look as though they were permanently affixed to the rib cage.

yourself to really *see* what is in front, alongside of, and behind you. Sometimes the casual habit of looking without really seeing can pose a safety hazard, as when riding across an open field with your mind decidedly elsewhere, your eyes looking but not seeing, and a gopher hole one step away; or in the show ring with another horse just waiting to kick either your horse or your leg, whichever happens to be there when his foot lands. However, if you can get into the habit of turning your head in the direction in which you wish to go and then looking *for* or *at* a particular destination or point while getting the general feel of what lies between you and it, chances are both you and your horse will arrive there safely and directly at least ninety-nine percent of the time.

When riding in groups such as in flat (or gaited) classes at horse shows or in the hunt field you must develop an awareness of what is happening around you without actually diverting your mind from the business of your own horse and where you are going. For instance, you might have noticed a big gray horse playing exceptionally hard in front of you and then find yourself forced to pass him. Getting around him should pose no problem because as long as you can see him, you will naturally choose the safest route around him. Once he is behind you however, you cannot forget him entirely and must keep an eye out for him and get the feeling of where he is, lest you wind up in a tight pocket with no place to go and the other horse breathing down your horse's tail. Again, this type of thing is not a part of your position as you ride, but rather an important aspect of the mental attitude or awareness you should create for yourself every time you throw a leg over a horse.

COMMON ERRORS

We have been talking about the ideal position and have pointed out that from this particular arrangement of the rider's body he is afforded the maximum control. Now let us take a few minutes to examine some of the more common mistakes and extremes in position to see how they affect the rider in terms of effective communication with and control over the horse. As before, we shall begin with the leg and the base and work our way up to the upper body, hands, and head.

Legs

The rider who favors a longer stirrup is infinitely better off than one who elects to ride short. In choosing the longer iron a rider may have to reach a bit for his stirrup, which could make it a little more difficult to keep his foot in the iron and possibly create a tendency to extend the toe downward instead of flexing the heel. These drawbacks might well be overlooked in light of the additional leg contact which is afforded by riding long. In fact, riding without stirrups is probably the best overall exercise for developing a strong and useful leg; it causes a rider to make his leg long and to get around the horse for a greater and decidedly closer feel of the animal. When a rider has been practicing without stirrups for a while, he usually finds that upon picking up his irons his leg feels somewhat cramped; he may discover that he has been riding too short. Indeed, it is not unusual for a rider to permanently lengthen his irons for flat work after extensive work without stirrups.

Riding short, on the other hand, requires a number of negative adjustments. For one, the rider who chooses to ride short is very likely to become perched upon his saddle and braced against his irons, developing a seat that resembles a jack-in-the-box. The knee has a natural springlike action that refuses to be unduly cramped for any length of time. When the stirrups are too short the rider is literally folded up like a telescope, and the knee begins to protest. Unable to relax the tension on it by extending the lower leg downward, it attempts to unfold itself upward, thus lifting the rider out of the saddle and perching him atop his horse. This lifting action in turn causes the rider to attempt to rectify his sudden divorce from the saddle by pushing or bracing his feet against the stirrup irons, which more often than not produces a temporary straightening of the knee and an abominable bouncing on the horse's back.

Another common method by which riders attempt to compensate for unduly short stirrups is the "legs on the dashboard" seat, in which the rider eases the pressure on his knees by throwing his legs as far forward as possible—often somewhere in the region of the horse's shoulder. Since it is virtually impossible to maintain one's balance in such a position, the rider is then forced to hunch his shoulders forward while his buttocks protrude behind him, forming a sort of counterbalance. The picture resulting from all these

Riding without stirrups is probably the best overall exercise for developing a strong and useful leg.

A rider must "make his leg long" and get his legs "around" the horse when riding without stirrups.

contortions is that of a rider who greatly resembles the letter "C"—
or a person suffering an acute appendicitis attack.

A person who winds up riding in such a position not only looks
somewhat desperate, but frequently he is, because he has greatly
limited his own flexibility. In this attitude, with his legs preceding
all other parts of the body, the rider finds that such simple moves
as posting to the trot or standing in the stirrups are hard work,
while cantering becomes a spine-jarring nightmare. No wonder!!
Every time the rider wishes to rise from the saddle or follow the
horse's forward motion he must first pull or push himself upward
and outward in order to get past his own knees. In this situation
the rider's body is working against him as he strains to move with
the horse. Try posting for ten minutes with your "legs on the dashboard"—you'll find that you become unusually uncomfortable and
fatigued before you're halfway through. As for cantering, it is very
difficult to soften your spine and absorb the concussion of the gait
when your legs and upper body come together at right angles at
your hip and are literally locked into this position.

Furthermore, with his "legs on the dashboard" a rider cannot
possibly use them to any avail (except of course, to nudge the horse
in the shoulder with a toe). Such a rider is not even in a position
to communicate with the horse's hindquarters, much less engage or
direct his hind legs in any sort of movement. By placing his feet
so far ahead of his body, the rider is voluntarily throwing away
the necessary equipment with which he could make his horse bend,
flex, lengthen, or shorten his stride or do any number of more complicated maneuvers—all of which require leg pressure and signals
emanating from the area just behind the girth.

The extreme opposite of riding with your "legs on the dashboard" is losing your leg behind you. In this instance, the rider's
knee becomes a pivot as the upper body and the thigh tip forward
past the knees while the lower leg and foot either slip or are flung
backward. In addition to the high incidence of this flaw on the
flat, you will find it occurs frequently with people who are beginning to jump, who feel they must leap forward upon the horse's
neck. A further bugaboo attached to the pivoting knee is the tendency for the toe to hang downward and the heel to be jerked upward, often catching the horse somewhere amidships and "goosing"
him unmercifully. It must also be noted that as the knee turns and

the upper body propels itself towards the horse's ears, the rider's body is no longer contained within a neat frame approximately in the middle of the animal's center of gravity. Instead, he is sprawled from one end of the horse to the other—arms reaching far out in front of him, legs slipping and sliding behind him—which can do much to disgruntle the most patient equine, not to mention unbalance the rider.

As is true with the "legs on the dashboard," a leg which is habitually carried excessively far behind the girth has the additional drawback of being only minimally effective for communication. There is seldom any strength in a leg that simply hangs from the knee. While it flops around from place to place, depending upon the degree of turning at the knee, it may also prove to be sufficiently annoying to the horse to act as a signal to "giddyap," which could seriously hamper one of the main lines of communication with the animal.

We have seen some of the complications that can arise from stirrups too long or too short and feet too far forward or too far back. There is a happy medium, however, which encompasses the ideal position and all its attendant variations. This position is available to anyone who is willing to work toward it. If you do not have the right feeling for the correct leg position, you may find it helpful to imagine a line beginning at the top of your shoulder which passes vertically through your hip and extends downward to touch the back of your heel. Although such a position would be difficult to maintain without any deviation, the usual result of this mental guideline is a leg which is as useful as it is ornamental.

Two extremely well-worn phrases are, at least in this writer's opinion, solely responsible for the most popular pair of misconceptions about the use of the leg. The first is "Grip with your knees!" and a close second, "Kick him to make him go!" We shall take them one at a time to reveal the worthlessness of each.

"Grip with your knees!"—mounted ad nauseam by nonriders who read fiction as well as riders who don't—undoubtedly had an origin somewhere, but certainly not in an area in which the hunter-seat (or any other type of English riding) was prevalent. Just the thought of gripping with one's knees is enough to push a knowledgeable hunter-seat rider inches out of the saddle! The more one tries to grip, grab, or squeeze with the knees, the more the base is

A *flopping leg, attached to a pivoting knee, can sometimes aggravate a horse. While the leg flops around from place to place, it may also prove to be sufficiently annoying to the horse to act as a signal to "giddyap," which could seriously hamper one of the main lines of communication.*

pushed upward and away from the saddle and the less likelihood for the lower leg to remain in contact with the horse's side. Since one of the main objects of hunter-seat, and indeed of all styles of English riding, is to get as close to the horse as possible (as opposed to the excellent advice of a well-known cutting horse trainer who, referring to the stock saddle, tells you in no uncertain terms to "Ride your saddle not your horse") any concept which in effect lengthens the distance between you and your horse should be disregarded.

"Kick him to make him go!" also fails, although there is some basis in truth for this well-known thought. Leg pressure ranging from a gentle squeeze to a dig with a spur means "go forward" to the average horse. Unfortunately the emphasis all too often rests on the word "kick," with the image of John Wayne flapping his legs into the sunset. Many fledgling riders attempt to do just that, and succeed in producing a resounding *"thwomp"* upon the horse's sides. The drawback in this is that in order to create a sufficiently hard "thwomp" it becomes necessary for the rider to stick his legs out to the side as far as possible before allowing them to fall. During those seconds in which the rider is poised with his leg (or legs if he is coordinated well enough to be using both at once) outstretched, he has, in effect, relinquished more than fifty percent of his control—the amount established by his legs—and simultaneously offered the horse a perfect opportunity to shy, swerve, or buck and thus catch his rider at a distinct disadvantage.

Trying to grip with the knees or kick with the feet are costly habits to get into, but there also exist a number of smaller, nuisance-type flaws by which you can easily cheat yourself of effective communication and control.

The rider who turns his toe out and only uses the back of his leg against the horse's side has only the surface area of the back of his legs available to communicate with his horse. Playing with half a deck, he is operating with a sizable handicap. He is missing half the punctuation marks necessary for a lively conversation with his mount, and is most likely criticizing the horse for failure to receive his signals. If he would turn his toe straight forward (or even a shade toward the inside) he would find a larger portion of his leg instantly in contact with the horse and would probably discover that his horse was much better than he had thought at getting messages straight.

Breaking the ankle toward the inside with the sole of the foot inclined toward the outside.

Another annoying habit is carrying the ankle in a cocked position—the ankle "breaking" toward the inside and the sole of that foot consequently turned toward the outside. This stems from a style of riding popular some years ago that advocated the definite inward flexion of the ankle as an aid to maintaining a stronger grip with the calf and the knee. Today's trends in riding are based upon the old Italian-style Fort Riley cavalry seat, which emphasizes the natural flow of the body and scarcely leaves room for a rigid ankle joint, or any other joint for that matter. The cocked position also proves to be something of a hindrance when it comes to closing your leg around a horse—since, by the very nature of its forced placement, the ankle and foot lack flexibility. A further faux pas directly related to this position is that you are far more apt to hit the horse with your leg unintentionally while attempting to maintain the correct placement.

Base

As we move our thoughts above the knee and consider the base, it might seem that all that is involved here is sitting in the saddle. Of course this is not the case, although there are fewer options available in the placement of the seat and thighs. One of the easiest habits to fall into is that of allowing the thighs to turn slightly outward and away from the saddle while trying to grip with the lower leg, calf, or heel. Certainly it is harder and more uncomfortable for a beginning rider to keep his thigh flat against the saddle, but the alternative loss of contact and sloppy position are doubly hard to correct once they become the accustomed style.

Another error is sitting too far back. It is much easier and less demanding upon the body muscles to plop oneself in the back of an English saddle and allow the legs to hang as they will. In this case, the rider will find himself faced with a seemingly endless uphill struggle to get with the motion of the horse. Furthermore, the deeper the seat on the saddle, the harder it is for the rider to follow the animal's movements from a backseat position. Therefore, although it requires a certain amount of concentration, the rider who is just beginning or attempting to correct his position should take care to place himself first in the *front* of his saddle and then securely upon his seat bones.

Upper Body

The upper body is open to countless faults due to the number of components involved and the variations peculiar to each individual. For instance, it is quite possible for a rider to carry his back straight as a ramrod, and yet have one shoulder noticeably higher or lower than the other, or perhaps incline his body so far forward as to ride in a plane parallel with the horse's neck. Rounded or uneven shoulders, a hunched back, a rigid neck, locked elbows or wrists, or inflexible hands can severely hamper if not wholly destroy the effectiveness of the upper body. Unfortunately, such habits as these can completely ruin the picture a rider presents. Although it is possible to get by with a well-positioned upper body accompanied by soft hands and a loose leg, it is virtually impossible to be forgiven for an upper body that is round-shouldered and doubled over, no matter how beautifully placed the lower leg may be.

There seems to be a universal tendency for beginning riders to hang draped over the horse's neck, leaning forward and downward in what appears to be an effort to be closer to the horse or, possibly, to the ground. Perhaps the idea of clutching the horse around the neck for security is not so far from the minds of most riders when faced with their first experience upon a horse's back. Whatever the reasoning behind it, it is a common mistake that, if made at the outset and allowed to continue, will result in a position that at best is most definitely out of balance. In addition to placing the rider in a situation from which it is practically impossible to apply his hands, weight, seat, or even his lower leg to any appreciable extent, this particular misplacement of the rider's upper body almost always produces an increase in the horse's speed. Remembering that the ideal position focuses on the horse's center of gravity, it stands to reason that any extreme shift in the rider's weight toward either the forehand or the hindquarters would upset the balance between the two and necessitate some measure of compensation. In this instance the animal feels the rider's weight out on his neck beyond his withers. He also feels a natural instinct to maintain his balance and would like to return the rider's weight to a position behind his withers, more nearly at his center of gravity. In order to do this he begins to increase his pace so as to get underneath the weight that is tipping his balance toward the front.

A round back can hamper the effectiveness of the upper body. Such habits as rounded or uneven shoulders, a hunched back, a rigid neck, locked elbows or wrists, or inflexible hands can completely ruin the picture a rider presents.

The "ideal" position focuses on the horse's center of gravity.

The farther forward the rider inclines his body the more the horse hurries to keep up,which, if the horse happened to be galloping instead of walking, could prove quite frightening to an unsure rider. Under such circumstances, if the rider were to return to an upright or vertical position (or even somewhat behind the vertical) he would be astounded at just how much braking action would be associated with such a simple body movement and how quickly he could regain control of the situation. Unfortunately it is not always so easy to think of the simple move that would save the day, particularly when you are under duress and your horse is even slightly out of hand. Sometimes it helps to keep in mind a picture of a race horse, running flat out with his jockey perched on his neck in the traditional "monkey on a stick" position—with the idea that you wish to do exactly the *opposite!* Everyone who has been around horses at all knows, furthermore, that most falls occur in a forward direction, over the horse's head, past either shoulder, and occasionally along either side. It is quite rare to see anyone catapulted straight upward out of the saddle or, even more curiously, off the back! So it would seem that the seats that are vertical or slightly behind the motion have at least one obvious advantage over those with a tendency to lean forward—namely, staying on.

What about leaning behind the vertical, or riding behind your leg? Just about the worst thing which can be said about this is that it does not present a particularly pleasing picture. If the rider leans too far back at all gaits, it tends to give the impression that his horse is unduly strong and that he is constantly fighting to hold him back. On the other hand, there are some instances in which the rider *ought* to be behind the vertical, as when riding a horse that sulks and does not want to move forward. In such a situation the horse is literally trying to back out from under his rider— perhaps looking for a chance to wheel and dart back to the stable, refuse to jump a fence, or commit some other disobedience. If the rider were to shift his weight or lean forward, the horse would be afforded the perfect opportunity to dig in his toes, prop and wheel, drop his shoulder, or try any trick by which he might successfully unseat the person on his back. If, however, the rider were to lean slightly back toward the horse's hips, deepen his seat, close his legs around the horse, and possibly lift his hands slightly (if the horse were prone to ducking), the animal would move forward in most cases and at least be thwarted in his attempts at contrariness

Leaning behind the vertical—riding behind your leg. Not a very pleasing picture!

in others. Under the circumstances just described, by the simple act of shifting his weight slightly behind the vertical, the rider enables himself to gain a deeper seat while adding strength to his lower back for the purpose of emphasizing his wish to go forward. Once the horse becomes aware of the rider's determination to move forward as expressed by the driving use of his seat and legs, he has very little choice other than to proceed in the direction indicated or be held at the point of his resistance while the rider employs stronger measures (i.e., the use of stick and/or spurs) until he complies.

Hands

Although the hands are a part of the upper body, their function and contribution to the overall success of any rider demand that they be treated separately. A rough, thoughtless, or insensitive set of hands can obliterate the studied use of seat and legs in minutes and at the same time cause a horse to become truculent, belligerent, or downright furious. The bars of a horse's mouth are one of the most sensitive parts of his body, and no matter how well-fitted or mild the bit might be, it still is a foreign device whose function is to direct and control the animal. To take the horse's viewpoint for a moment, it is bad enough to be expected to tolerate a piece of metal or hard rubber in your mouth without having to endure the further discomfort of steady pressure, sudden snatches, inflexibility, or any combination thereof.

Perhaps the easiest habit to acquire and the hardest to break is that of hanging onto the horse's mouth. It is the natural inclination or reaction of many riders in the early learning stages, particularly those who are somewhat timid and seem to derive a feeling of security from shortening the reins unnecessarily and really pulling on the horse's mouth. Most horses resent this steady pressure on their gums and after a while begin to lean against it. Thus begins a vicious circle in which the more the rider shortens and tightens his hold, the more the horse bears down on the bit until the rider finds himself literally holding up the weight of the animal's entire forehand. Once a horse has learned the unpleasant defense of "lugging on the bit" he is quite apt to do it without provocation just on the chance that the rider *might* take a hold of him. It is equally difficult for riders who have ridden a number of horses that pull to believe that this one is different or has a very soft mouth and light-

Once a horse has learned the unpleasant defense of "lugging on the bit" he is quite apt to do it without provocation. The horse here leans on his rider's hands while she "softens" her hand in an effort to give him "nothing to lug against."

en their hold accordingly. All too often they think that maintaining a death-grip on the reins is synonymous with control. The actual result of this hanging-on is that they lose the horse's willingness to be helpful and cooperative.

On the other hand, it is just as much a mistake to ride a horse using a loose, flopping rein as it is to choke him to death. He, naturally, is less likely to pick a fight about an overly loose rein; but any gain you might make in not antagonizing him, you lose through lack of communication. For one thing, it is extremely difficult to direct a horse with an excessively long rein. Furthermore, it robs him of the comfort and support afforded by a light feel of his mouth, reassuring him that he is being held together and in balance. There are few horses who do not benefit from a light, supporting touch and many who come to depend upon it. Take it away and a horse may become strung out of balance—stumbling frequently and heavy on his forehand. Fortunately for both horse and rider, it is much easier to correct a passive hand than one that has become overly strong or aggressive. Although all that is required in either case is enlightenment as to exactly how the hands ought to be used and what response should be expected from the horse, it is considerably more difficult to unlearn a fixed habit and re-educate oneself to a whole new outlook than to learn to use something that has never been used before in any fashion.

Everyone has seen, at one time or another, a horse that was misbehaving in some way—refusing to turn in a certain direction, flexing his chin on his chest and running fast but not out of control, standing obstinately and refusing to budge—and a rider who was yanking abusively on the reins to no avail. Such spectacles continually emphasize the fact that in a sport in which so much depends upon the educated hands of the rider, there should be no tolerance at all for the ignorant brutalization of the animal's mouth. A rider's failure to get his message across to the horse by what he considers conventional methods is no justification for cruelty. The only certain result of such an outburst is a high-headed, fearful creature that is far more concerned with when the next jolt in the mouth will occur than what it is he is supposed to be doing or even where he is about to put his feet. This is not to imply that an occasional pinch on the reins to bring a horse's head up from between his knees or to lift him from lugging is not perfectly in order, but to

Riding a horse on a loose, flopping rein can cause him to become "strung out," out of balance and heavy on his forehand.

make clear the difference between the calculated use and wanton misuse of a rider's hands.

Just as some people are gifted in the field of music and their fingers dance across the keys and strings with unbelievable dexterity, so are some people blessed with an instinctive feel for a horse's mouth. Those who are not born with this inherent sensitivity but still wish to ride seriously must develop their skills to the utmost and rely more on their training than their natural ability. It is not enough, for example, to learn where to put your hands at the canter if the fingers holding the reins are tightened into a fist and there is no give with the bobbing motion of the horse's head. So, in order to insure that the horse is neither working against fixed or rigid hands nor bouncing off the bit at every stride, the rider must consciously practice softening his hands to allow such freedom of movement as is necessary until the action becomes mechanical and requires no forethought at all. The effect of a heavy-handed rider is one of constant discouragement and/or punishment to the horse, regardless of the intent. It is important, therefore, to overcome this deficiency.

In addition to those serious habits of hands that are guaranteed to involve and irritate the horse, there are also a few that have little direct bearing upon the horse but can do much to hamper communication and control. The horse will turn, for example, to whichever side he feels a pull on his bit, regardless of how the rider managed to do it. It is more effective, however, to signal by drawing the entire right arm back toward the body than to give a little tug by bending the wrist. The horse doesn't mind if you bend your wrists or hold your hands with the thumbs facing each other; but you will find it easier to do what you have to do with your elbows in, your wrists straight, and your thumbs up.

Similarly, it does not appear that the horse particularly cares whether his rider carries his hands too high or too low as long as the meaning of the signal is clear and it is not given in an abusive manner. However, a rider who is working to improve his position will find it difficult to progress if his hands are not in the right place from the start. Here it is the rider who discovers that if his hands are too high he has difficulty staying soft and fluid and that if they are too low it is hard to keep from nagging the horse.

Head and Eyes

In any discussion of riding position and technique, having a good head on your shoulders is particularly apt in the literal sense. "Good," in this instance, means "well-placed"; nothing can detract more quickly from a rider's overall appearance than poor head carriage or a sullen facial expression. It may take a judge or spectator a few minutes to discern the flaws in a leg, seat, or hands, but the reaction to the look upon your face and the way you hold your head is almost instantaneous.

A stiff neck and leading chin immediately give the impression of complete rigidity and, while it is not always the case, a prominent chin usually indicates little or no natural movement of the head. In addition, the forward thrust of the lower jaw seems to draw the entire upper body forward with it in a somewhat tilted or overhanging position. It also follows that if the head does not move, the eyes are limited to a field of vision that includes only the area directly in front of them.

A hanging head is just as damaging to the overall picture as a preceding chin since the general impression imparted is one of weakness, incompetence, or even fright. It is not unusual for a hanging head to disappear somewhere into the rider's shoulders, all but eclipsing his neck and largely resembling a turtle withdrawn into his shell. From such a position there is little for the eyes to behold except for the ground and the horse's feet, neither of which is conducive to planning ahead. This more than likely provided the basis for the saying "People who look down end up on the ground!"

Fortunately, neither head problem is particularly difficult to correct. Usually it is just a matter of discipline and concentration—reaching for the inside of your shirt collar with the back of your neck, or practicing any number of simple eye exercises, until using your head (and eyes as well) becomes a habit.

Thus far we have discussed the lower leg, thigh, seat, upper body, hands, and head in light of the more common problems related to each as well as with reference to their ideal placement. We know how the position is supposed to look and we also have a pretty fair idea why it seldom does. We know that there are principles we can follow to make riding easier, and there are pitfalls by which we make our own stumbling blocks.

The rider here demonstrates a stiff neck and the accompanying "leading chin" position.

EXERCISES

There is no one magic word to sum up the requirements for success in riding, but if there were it would probably be "relaxation." Tension has no place in the body or mind of a serious rider, for not only does it inhibit his natural ability to flow with the horse's motion, but it also is instantly transmitted to the horse. Relaxation is the outgrowth of confidence, and the surest way to develop confidence in yourself as a rider is by establishing a firm foundation of riding skills so that you have a secure seat and maximum control of both yourself and the horse.

How do you improve your skills? The answer is practice, *practice*, PRACTICE!!! This does not mean jumping on your horse for ten or twenty minutes per day and riding around the ring, fields, or cross country at whatever gait happens to suit your mood or the horse's whim at the time. The kind of practice that is needed follows a similar pattern each day, beginning with simple exercises for both horse and rider and working up to whatever level the two of you have reached. There is no short cut by which a pianist can bypass his scales and still play a piece; neither is there an easy way to ride effectively without first learning how to use your body. At this point we should realize that we are not talking about the once-a-week pleasure rider who asks no more of himself and his horse than that they enjoy a walk or canter through the woods on alternate Tuesdays and Saturdays. This type of rider (as well as those who ride for the diversion or the exercise) rarely concerns himself with the level to which his riding skill has progressed. Since he has no interest in causing his horse to perform in a certain manner at a given time, he also has no need to do anything more than sit on a horse and go along for the ride.

Let us assume then, that we are dealing with a serious-minded student who wishes to make the most of his riding abilities and is willing to devote a fair amount of time to that end. How should he allocate his time? What are realistic goals toward which he can work? How should he measure his progress?

One of the most important points to remember when undertaking any sport is that you cannot possibly become proficient at it overnight. This is particularly true when riding. Even if you were able to ride for two hours a day, seven days per week, it would take the better part of a year for you to become relatively accomplished on the flat, and then only on a well-schooled horse. All too often people become impatient at their seeming lack of progress, and when everything doesn't fall into place immediately they tend to lose interest. With the exception of fear, loss of interest is the most damaging mental attitude that can befall a would-be rider. To ride well you must be vitally interested in anything that concerns you or your horse. You must be curious as to how and why the animal responds in one way to your hand and in another to your leg. You must at sometime wonder "what would happen if . . ." and most certainly try at least once to discover whether you can make him do the same things you saw that other person doing. A little variety or an occasional challenge is helpful and pleasurable for both horse and rider; nevertheless, it is wise to remember that you can get a great deal of enjoyment and satisfaction from the learning process itself if you try not to expect too much too soon.

Every riding hour might be broken into three parts as follows: first, ten minutes of warm-up and suppling exercises for both horse and rider; second, twenty minutes of more advanced exercises designed to improve the rider's position; third, thirty minutes of patterns, exercises, and work at all gaits, some for the horse's benefit and some for the rider.

There are literally thousands of exercises to perform and patterns to ride, certainly enough so that you need never repeat the same ones more than twice a week. All are bound to help you or your horse in some way or another. However, it is not a good idea to try to execute those specifically intended to improve your position without the benefit of supervision. This is mainly because it is very easy to unconsciously move one part of your body during an exercise in which a different part is moving deliberately, and in so doing create a new problem. It is also unwise to engage in the more difficult exercises to the point of fatigue, again because you are apt to do more harm than good in your efforts to perfect the exercise when your body is tired.

Legs

As far as exercises for the legs and leg positions are concerned, although there are numerous suppling movements that can be employed to relax a tense or rigid leg—such as rotating the ankles, feet, or entire lower leg—the most effective and beneficial exercise that you can do to strengthen your leg is to ride without stirrups. As with any other exercise, you must take care not to ride without your irons for too long a time in the beginning lest you become overly tired and clutch at the saddle with your knees, hang your toes, or develop such undesirable habits as heaving your shoulders up and down or balancing on the horse's mouth.

Upper Body

1. Bend down and touch the left toe with the left hand and the right toe with the right hand.

2. Bend down and twist so as to touch the left toe with the right hand and the right toe with the left hand.

3. Rotate the arms in full circles from the shoulder, first right then left, then both arms together.

4. Bend forward and touch the horse's mane with your nose without using your hands.

5. Lean all the way back over the cantle of the saddle until your head is resting on the horse's croup.

6. Touch your right or left knee with your nose.

7. Extend your arms from the shoulders either straight up or out to the sides—right, left, then both together.

8. Reach straight ahead with one hand to touch the horse's neck and then reach straight back to touch his croup.

9. Twist around to touch your right hand to the horse's left side and then your left hand to his right side.

10. Ride with arms crossed in front of your chest, elbows away from the body.

Head, Neck, and Eyes

1. Shrug your shoulders from time to time (this means making a conscious effort to do so) to keep from setting your head.

2. Ride a circle around a person or object while keeping your eyes fixed on that person or object.

3. Make right and left turns from a straight line, being sure to turn your head so that your eyes precede the turn.

4. Touch your chin first to your right shoulder and then to your left shoulder while riding in a straight line.

5. Reach for the back of your shirt collar with the back of your neck to keep from stretching your head forward or hunching your shoulders.

Balance

1. Extend the right foot as far forward as possible while reaching the left foot back. Then reverse.

2. Bring both feet forward and up together so that your heels click over the horse's neck. Then, leaning forward, bring them back and up so that they touch over the horse's croup.

3. With your arms folded across your chest, turn completely around in the saddle, alternating first one way and then the other. Your legs should cross in front of you when turning.

4. Stand in the saddle and then rest all your weight on your hands as you slowly resume your seat.

Flying Dismounts

Flying dismounts at the walk, trot, and canter can do much to dispel the usual uneasiness associated with falling and thereby give the rider a greater sense of security. For this exercise you should begin at the standstill. Take both feet from the stirrups and place your hands on the horse's neck. Then lean forward with your weight resting briefly on your hands and swing your legs out behind you, clearing the saddle as you spring down. At the same time push yourself slightly away from the horse's neck so that you land alongside his shoulder, on your feet, keeping hold of the reins. When dismounting in this fashion from the trot and canter you must be prepared to run a few steps with the horse until he stops, unless he has been trained to halt the moment your feet touch ground.

Half-Seat Position

The half-seat, hand gallop position, jumping position, and seat are but a few of the names commonly applied to the rider's posi-

A proper execution of the half-seat. The half-seat is the correct position when riding to a jump.

tion when approaching a jump. It has not been included in the examples of general exercises mainly because, while it doubles as an excellent exercise for improving balance and for getting weight in the heels, it functions primarily as the correct position for the rider approaching a fence. Since the half-seat, as we shall call it, is *the* correct position when riding to a jump, it is particularly important that it be executed correctly. For this reason it is better not to begin working on your half-seat until your legs are somewhat under control and your balance is at least partially established at the walk, trot, and canter. Furthermore, it is a good idea to have someone watch you in your first attempts at the half-seat because it is so easy to compensate for a seemingly uncomfortable feeling by falling into a bad habit or, worse yet, to create a totally incorrect position simply because there was no one present to tell you how it looked. It does not take a knowledgeable horseman or instructor to tell you that you look round-shouldered, straight-legged, or as if you were lying on the horse's neck—that your legs are either too far in front of you or too far behind you—or that they think you are about to fall off over the horse's tail. Anyone who is willing to spend the time watching you when you ride can learn to recognize what the ideal position should look like and then tell you what *you* look like in comparison.

The half-seat when practiced on the flat is no different from the half-seat used in jumping, except that there is neither a move to follow the horse's head and neck movement (as when he stretches out or arcs over a fence) nor the barely perceptible additional transfer of weight onto your knees and into your heels, which are the natural extensions of the half-seat as the horse leaves the ground.

In order to find a working half-seat you begin by sitting in the proper position at the standstill. Then, inclining your body slightly forward, place your hands on either side of the horse's neck about four to six inches in front of his withers and tip your weight off your pelvic bones, onto your knees, and into your heels. You should make a particular effort to stay over the horse's center of gravity, which in this case means over the middle of the saddle, and to drop down and around your horse as you place more weight in your heels. With practice you should be able to assume and maintain your half-seat at all gaits and, for the utmost benefit to your overall balance and security, without the use of reins.

Gaits

Before moving on to the more advanced gymnastics and suppling exercises involving the horse as well as the rider, let us take a look at the gaits at which these maneuvers are performed. There can be no promptness or precision in the execution of a serpentine at the canter, for example, if the gait itself lacks cadence and uniformity. By the same token, a lackluster, shambling excuse for a trot is a sure sign that the rider is not in control of the horse or is making no attempt to improve the gait. On the other hand, a somewhat haphazard figure eight may appear to be better than it actually is simply because the horse's gaits are animated and well defined. Furthermore, the perfection of a good walk, trot and canter is an exercise in itself.

WALK

Unfortunately the walk is all too often treated as little more than a necessary phase through which one must pass while on the way to something else, or the ultimate "home" to which one must return regardless of where they've been or what they must do to

60

get back there. This is hardly the case. The walk is definitely a gait in its own right, with varied degrees of excellence in its execution. Performed properly, the walk should be neither too fast nor too slow—that is, not so forced or rapid as to be on the verge of or interspersed with jogging steps, but not so sluggish and weighty as to seem hesitant and lacking animation.

Because walking is an excellent exercise in which the horse uses every part of his body, he should be encouraged to develop a free-moving, flat-footed stride in which he proceeds directly forward without deviation or wandering from side to side. His steps should be purposeful and his mind alert to his rider's demands with regard to changes of pace and direction and his surroundings—in that order! This is not to imply that there are not times when the horse should be allowed complete freedom to relax and just amble on a loose rein around the ring or across a field or down a trail, but these times should be reserved for the end of the work period, after a particularly difficult exercise before proceeding to the next, or on the horse's "day off."

In order to produce a *gait* rather than an aimless shuffle the rider himself must be attentive to the business at hand and not stop riding just because he's walking. He should be well-positioned in the saddle, sitting tall, making his leg as long and his upper body as tall as possible. With his leg placed correctly against the horse's sides slightly behind the girth and his hands soft and sensitive, he should be able to detect or feel any increase or decrease in speed as well as any tendency to wander or drift from an intended line, and correct it before it becomes apparent to an onlooker.

For instance, if the horse happens to be particularly heavy on his front end—that is, pulling against the rider's hands and more or less bulling his way forward—the rider should take measures to correct and lighten his forehand *before* he either breaks into a jog or begins choosing his own directions. The rider can successfully run interference in such a situation by slipping his pelvis slightly forward while squeezing his legs and lightly lifting his hands. What he is doing, in essence, is picking the horse up off its forehand with his hands while, with his legs and seat, he is forcing the horse to accept this directive by not allowing him to back away from it, and causing the animal to return to a better balanced position by bringing the hindquarters in underneath him.

For the rider who is having a problem or is learning something new, the old cliche "You must walk before you can run" bears a worthwhile message. With your legs or hands in place, practice the movement at the walk, making either a figure eight or a halt, a serpentine or a circle. Continue until the movement is yours at that gait, then move on to the trot, canter, and hand gallop. You will be surprised how much easier everything is at the faster gaits when you have done your "homework" at the walk, and conversely how everything becomes so much more difficult when speed is added to an exercise that is not yet under control at the walk.

POSTING TROT

The ordinary posting trot is probably the best single exercise for the overall conditioning of the horse as well as being a good ground-covering gait. A horse that has been out of work for some time can be conditioned faster by working at the trot than by spending the same amount of time at any other gait. When a horse trots properly he uses his whole body in a lively, springy, two-beat gait of unalterable rhythm. He carries himself in balance, with his shoulders rotating freely and his feet gliding forward, not upward, with each step. His hind legs should reach well underneath his body to provide the utmost impulsion, or drive, while his front legs should swing out from the shoulder and complete their stride with the hoof landing squarely upon the ground.

When posting, the rider should try to stay light on the horse's back, allowing the action of the trot to throw him up and then returning to his seat softly so as not to land in the saddle with a thud. In order to maintain a steady cadence, the rider must be particularly sensitive to the horse's tendencies to fall back or surge forward, and must be quick to react accordingly.

Posting to the trot also necessitates paying attention to "diagonals." When a horse trots he moves his feet forward in diagonal pairs. If you are rising from the saddle as the right foreleg leaves the ground, you are posting on the *left* diagonal; if you are rising from the saddle as the left foreleg leaves the ground, you are riding on the *right* diagonal. When riding cross country or without particular direction, it is not essential to look at your diagonals for any purpose other than to change occasionally so as not to tire the

At the trot, the horse carries himself in balance, deriving his impulsion from his hindquarters while his forelegs swing freely from the shoulder, completing their stride with the hoof landing squarely upon the ground.

horse's back or make him overly strong on one side. However, when you are working in small circles, such as when practicing figures of eight or riding inside a ring where the horse is turning frequently, the matter of correct and incorrect diagonals requires your attention.

The correct diagonal to use on a turn or circle is the one that corresponds with the direction in which the horse is traveling. When the horse is moving left, for example, the left diagonal should be used. Since the right foreleg is on the outside in this instance, it must cover more ground and, therefore, work harder than the left foreleg. The rider should time his posting, therefore, so as to facilitate the momentum of the outside leg—rising as the right foreleg leaves the ground and moves forward, sitting as it moves toward the ground. It is this action of moving with the *outside* foreleg that determines what is correct and incorrect with respect to diagonals. In other words, if you are rising from the saddle as the outside foreleg moves forward you are on the correct diagonal; but, if you are rising with the inside foreleg and *sitting* in the saddle as the outside foreleg moves forward, you are incorrect.

SITTING TROT

The sitting trot should be somewhat slower than the posting trot but should maintain every bit as much life and animation as the posting trot. Since the rider is accepting all the concussion of the gait with his body he should try to absorb as much of the shock as possible with his lower back and avoid tensing his seat muscles. It is a great deal easier to "get a leg on a horse" from a sitting trot than from a posting trot because the rider is in constant contact with the animal rather than moving about. He also has full use of his seat to encourage the horse to move forward, which is out of the question when posting.

Like the walk, the sitting trot is a particularly valuable tool for solving problems that arise for both the horse and rider. For example, if a horse is having trouble bending around his turns or a rider just can't seem to keep from slipping his leg out in front of him at the ordinary trot, he will more than likely find his difficulties are permanently over after working them out at the sitting trot and then proceeding to post. In addition to the overall increase in effectiveness of the rider's seat and legs that seems to be the

Posting on the correct diagonal while moving counterclockwise. The rider rises from the saddle as the outside foreleg moves forward.

Posting on the incorrect diagonal while moving counterclockwise. The rider is sitting in the saddle as the outside fore-leg moves forward. The sitting trot should maintain as much life and animation as the posting trot.

"hidden" feature of the sitting trot, it also is an excellent balance builder. Practicing this gait without stirrups is still another exercise guranteed to tighten your seat and improve your legs at the same time.

CANTER

While there is nothing more comfortable to sit to than the rocking-chair canter of a well-balanced horse who maintains a steady pace, there is nothing more *un*comfortable and spine-jarring than the canter of an ill-balanced horse who proceeds forward in fits and starts, alternately lugging on his rider's hands and spitting out the bit as the mood strikes him.

Cadence, rhythm, call it what you will, this is the key to the canter. Unfortunately the average horse is not inclined to fall into a pulsing one-two-three beat at the drop of a hat, and so it is up to the rider to establish the rate of speed and then keep it. There is also the matter of leads to be considered, and since the successful maintenance of rhythm depends largely upon good balance and self-carriage, there is little that can be done until correct leads are a matter of course.

Because a horse tends to seek his own natural balance, you will find that he will be on the correct lead in a given direction a large percentage of the time. Therefore, the problem facing the rider is not one of showing the animal the advantage of being correct, but rather of establishing a system of communication that will produce the desired lead *every* time. To this end, there are two more widely accepted signals. While each involves pressure from the leg opposite to the desired lead simultaneous with a slight tension on the rein, they differ as to which rein is to be pulled. In one version the rein opposite to the lead is used, in the second it is the rein on the same side. To ask for a *left* lead, then, you would use a right leg in combination with either rein, depending on which type of signal the horse has been trained to respond to. Of course, there are many variations of these two methods—such as using only hand or only leg signals, or sometimes a voice command—but these are the result of individual training and choice.

Regardless of the hand and leg combination which is used, the rider must take care to indicate his wishes to the horse with as

little motion as possible. He should pay strict attention to his upper body, for there seems to be a universal tendency among eques-
trians in the learning stages to hurl their bodies forward in an effort
to throw their mount into the gait and onto the lead. This is completely wrong. If anything, it robs the rider of the use of his seat
at a time when the closer contact would work to his advantage in
encouraging the animal to move forward from its quarters. In addition, a sudden shift of the rider's weight toward the horse's neck
and shoulders is apt to cause the horse to become heavy on his
forehand just at the moment when he ought to be extremely light
in front in order to begin cantering. It stands to reason that a horse
cannot be expected to respond promptly to a signal for a gait char-
acterized by a back-to-front rocking motion when his forehand is
buried in the ground and his hindquarters are strung out behind
him somewhere. He also cannot be expected to strike out on the
correct lead if he has just placed the foot he ought to lead with on
the ground.

In order to avoid these common pitfalls, it is important to ask
your horse to canter at a time when he is most likely to answer
immediately with the correct lead and in such a way that he is
actually aided by your signal to do the correct thing. Although this
may sound like a complicated set of instructions, all that is required is a little common sense coupled with a heightened awareness
of the animal's gait. If you make it a habit to think about the lo-
cation of your horse's feet just prior to asking him to canter, soon
you will be able to feel when he is about to pick up the foot you
want him to lead with and time your signal to coincide with this
event. Or, if every time you think about cantering you "gather"
your horse together and make sure he is working from your leg to
your hand, he *must* be light. After a while you won't have to think
about gathering him together to canter; instead you will feel for
the coiling spring action that indicates that your horse is in good
balance with his hindquarters underneath him.

Once you have become accustomed to feeling for the most propi-
tious moment to ask for the canter, when you are able to feel the
exact moment when your horse is in the best natural balance from
which to proceed forward, you are ready to learn how to give him
the signal. As you do not wish to throw him out of balance or
make a move that would force him to react in an extreme manner,

Trying to "throw" a horse into the can-
ter can cause the rider to "lose" his up-
per body. It robs the rider of the use of
his seat at a time when the closer contact
would work to his advantage in encour-
aging the animal to move forward from
its quarters.

the obvious solution is to ask in the quietest way possible. Making sure that your weight is well situated upon your seat bones and the upper body quietly in position, squeeze with the opposite leg to indicate the lead you want, and close the fingers a little tighter on the rein to produce a slight, tension-type signal. A swift kick in the ribs or a good yank on the reins would be most inadvisable.

After your horse has broken on the correct lead it is your job to tell him how fast or slow you want him to go and then to maintain that rate of speed. Some horses tend to leap into their canter much like a racehorse breaking from the starting gate and then pick up speed with each stride. Others are sluggish at the start and tend to hang back with every step. Unless you are riding a horse that is a veritable machine, it is more than likely you will face either one or both of these problems in varying degrees and combinations.

Since your goal at the canter is establishing and maintaining an even, rhythmic gait, you cannot allow the horse to deviate from this cadence except to answer your signal for a lengthened or shortened stride. If he bears down with his head and shoulders and increases his pace, you will get the feeling that you are rushing downhill. To counteract this uncomfortable feeling and return your horse to proper balance, you should lift your hands slightly to raise his head, deepen your seat and apply your legs to make sure that he is pushed into your hand and forced to listen, and shift your weight slightly toward his hindquarters (inclining your shoulders toward his hips is a good way to think of it) as you drive him into your hand with your seat.

If, on the other hand, your horse is decidedly reluctant to keep cantering and is either just hanging back or so strung out that his canter produces a four-beat rhythm interspersed with trotting steps (particularly behind) you have to work a little harder. In such a situation not only must you hold the horse together by the determined use of a driving seat and definite leg to force him into your hand, but you also must compel him to maintain his forward motion by the even stronger use of your seat and legs while your hands remain sympathetic enough not to discourage him from moving into them yet firm enough to provide a degree of support.

Learning to make a horse canter the way *you* want him to, in a cadence that flows from one stride to the next, is a challenge. It forces the rider to demand and yield, be soft yet firm, use legs, seat, hands, and weight interchangeably and/or simultaneously to compensate for even the slightest change *before* it happens so that the final picture is one of fluid motion from start to finish.

It is important to remember that whenever you ride, be it just at the walk, trot, and canter or in intricate circle, lines, and programs punctuated by transitions and changes of direction, everything you do and each move you make will communicate something to the horse. If your position is correct then your body will function correctly and thus produce the correct movements of the horse. William Steinkraus explains this clearly in his book *Riding and Jumping*, ". . .all our most effective means of initiating and controlling the horse's movement depend on a sound position; and it is only by utilizing these means that we can get our horse to move properly, and in turn carry us properly so that our correct position can be effortlessly maintained."

He further points out "If the horse's defenses—say a stiff back and rough gaits—can force us to compromise the soundness of our position, then we will have permitted him to rob us of our only means of penetrating those defenses."

You might also bear in mind that the horse's position at the time when he is asked to perform a particular movement determines the ease, difficulty, or complete impossibility of such an action. For example, a horse cannot be expected to make his back round when jumping a fence if his head is stuck up in the air over his back as he leaves the ground, nor can he be expected to break off at the canter on the left lead if he is standing on his left front foot when he is asked.

As your riding skills progress and your working patterns become more varied and complicated, it is helpful to think of your horse's body as being contained within an imaginary frame. This frame encompasses a well-balanced horse who carries himself independently instead of leaning on his rider; his hindquarters swing forward with every step providing all the motive power he ever needs. In order for the horse to put up a resistance or attempt to evade his rider's directions, as in boring against the bit and forcing the rider to support his forehand or poking his head into the air and dropping behind the bit, he must fall out of the frame. Therefore, while it would be an oversimplification to say that keeping a horse in frame eliminates all problems, it is certainly a great aid in gaining control. By getting the horse to work off of its hindquarters, the rider gains control of his mount's hind legs and consequently of the horse itself.

Gymnastics

There is much to be gained by both horse and rider from a concentrated effort to improve and develop the horse's gáits. It is unfair, nevertheless, to expect either one to maintain a high degree of interest in what he is doing if the daily program consists of nothing more than a constant repetition of walk, trot, and canter around the edge of a ring. Such monotony will lead to sheer boredom on the part of both horse and rider. The result will be a disinterested, stumbling animal that is looking for distractions and excuses to misbehave, and a daydreaming, mind-wandering person who is reacting mechanically to the horse's motion while performing his own mental gymnastics in a completely different field.

Conversely, a riding program that is generously flavored with circles, serpentines, figures of eight, (or seven, or three—whatever happens to strike your fancy) half-halts, leg yielding, and transitions, will keep your horse guessing and alert to the slightest indication of change. It also provides you with an opportunity to exercise your mind while plotting the next course and trying to stay at least one jump ahead of your equine partner. Of course all patterns can and should be executed at the walk, sitting trot, posting trot, and canter. You have to realize that in order to perform a specific exercise well at the canter, you must first be fairly competent at performing it at the walk and trots.

PROGRAMMED RIDES

Since there are so many exercises and unlimited combinations with which a rider can vary his daily plan, let's take a sampling and see what is expected of the horse and of the rider, what problems can arise, and how they might be solved.

Circle

Circles are incorporated so frequently into the average ride that it is sometimes difficult to think of them as valuable tools of the rider and indispensable training devices for the horse. Executed properly, a circle can help a "green" horse find his balance; teach a stiff horse how to bend his body, thus rendering him more supple; restore control to the rider of an unusually strong horse that has "taken over" or is threatening to; help a rider learn to steer his horse and prepare him for more complicated maneuvers; and demonstrate the effectiveness of the rider's hand, leg, and overall control. It may also be used as a punishment device. For example, in the case of a horse who is trying to evade his rider's signal to proceed forward by running to the right, the horse might be spun abruptly around to the left and thereby returned to his original position.

The catch to making a circle is making it round! It should not have corners or lines, nor should it be elliptical, oval, or angular in shape. The rider should begin at a designated point and proceed forward on a curve until he reaches that point again. Since a near miss in the case of a circle is the same as a mile, the rider must be careful to have a marked point for beginning and ending a circle. The horse's body is arranged, at least theoretically, in a straight line (although simple "crookedness" of his spinal column is one of the animal's favorite forms of resistance). It is not an easy matter, therefore, to just put him on a circle and have him follow it. A firm control is required to create a figure that has a definite center and a perimeter consistently equidistant from that center. Pseudo-circles

A horse "bending" in the direction of his circle.

Resisting a circle, the horse drops his shoulder to the inside, lifts his head, and throws his haunches toward the outside of the circle.

that are three-quarters round and one-quarter flat, pointed or otherwise, are all too often allowed to pass for the real thing. This slipshoddiness only results in horses that do not know how to bend and riders who do not know how to make them.

Once a horse has learned to make his body work *for* him on a circle, he will find it infinitely easier to handle himself on any turn, be it on the flat or a part of a jumping course. By the same token, once a rider has learned how to make a horse bend in the direction of his circle he is well equipped to move on to the challenge of more advanced configurations. It follows that the tighter the turn the more difficult its execution, and the greater the speed, the less time available for adjustments or correction. Nonetheless, when a rider really knows how to make a horse bend he has a veritable skeleton key at his disposal.

Unfortunately the average beginning rider will make his first attempts at circling into a sort of tug-of-war with the horse's mouth. Leaning forward with one arm extended in a sort of leading fashion or leaning back and trying to tow the beast around are equally unsuccessful. Both are seen all too often. Instead, the rider would be far better off if he forgot about his reins as far as the actual turning of the horse is concerned and concentrated upon his legs and seat. To be sure, he will wish to use his hands lightly to indicate the direction in which he wishes to circle, but he should bear in mind that the horse is propelled from the rear and is far more apt to be influenced by the rider's weight, seat, and legs than by his hands. Hand signals can be answered by the simple ruse of rubber-necking (turning only the head while the body proceeds as before).

Let us assume that our rider is well positioned on his horse and is planning to circle to the left. Remember that the main objective is to create a truly round circle—not an octagon or pentagon. Either might be the result if the horse were unwilling to bend. In order to trace a fluid, circular path, the horse's head, shoulder, and haunch must be aligned on the curve. He may not deviate from this path by dropping his shoulder to the inside; by sticking his head up and extending it either straight in front of him or out to one side or the other; or by throwing his haunches toward the outside of the circle. In fact, in order to produce such an alignment at all, it is necessary for the horse to literally bend in the middle, make a curve out of his ribs, and then place his neck, shoulder, and haunch accordingly.

It is here, at the strategic bend in the middle, that the rider wins or loses his circle. If he is vague and half-hearted about asking his horse to bend, then his circle will be indefinite and shapeless. If, on the other hand, he shifts his weight slightly onto his left seat bone and applies his inside leg (in this case the left) just about at the girth, he is establishing a definite "center post" around which his horse may work. (This "inside leg at the girth" acts as a sort of crease in the horse's side that forces him to bend, prevents him from falling to the inside of the circle, and all the while provides a hub and guidepost for his circle.) The rider should then drop his outside leg (the right) slightly behind the girth, where it will serve the dual purpose of insuring that the horse *does* bend around the inside leg and indicating to the horse the demand for forward motion. Placing the outside leg behind the girth forces the horse to move his haunches toward the center of the circle, thus holding the horse around the rider's inside leg and preventing him from drifting toward the outside. This leg, together with the rider's seat, also calls for continuous forward motion.

Although the stronger signals emanate from the rider's seat and legs, the hands and upper body are not idle. For a left turn the rider draws his left hand straight back toward his body by bending his elbow. It is important that the inside of his arm pass easily along his side. This avoids the stilted or stiff-armed appearance of the rider who tries too hard to keep his arms close to his body and winds up with his elbows practically touching in front of him. The right hand should soften to compliment the pressure being brought to bear by the left rein and to *allow* the horse to turn his head slightly, so that the animal's left eye can be seen without leaning forward or changing position. The upper body shifts slightly in the direction of the circle—the rider's inside (left) shoulder inclined toward the horse's inside (left) *hip*—not forward over the animal's shoulder as is frequently, albeit erroneously, the case.

At the slower gaits (the walk and sitting trot) and/or when working in relatively large areas (such as one-half or one-quarter of the ring) the rider will find that really round circles can be accomplished with almost minimal effort once the principles are fully understood and applied. It quickly becomes apparent, however, that smaller areas and/or increases in speed require more thought and action on the rider's behalf. The reasons here are obvious but worthy of note. First, the tighter the circle the more the horse must bend to complete it evenly and the more likely he is to fall into the center or drift to the outside to escape the demands being placed upon him. Second, as the rider begins to make circles at the posting trot and canter, things happen much more quickly than at the walk. For example, if the horse starts to drop a shoulder, bears right or left, refuses to turn, or offers some other form of resistance, there is less available time in which to correct him. It is then possible for him to get away with more nonsense than when he is moving slowly. Third, and last, the matter of increased speed requires transmitting additional information to the horse. For instance, if you wish to make a circle at the canter, not only must you organize and communicate your message to make a circle, but you must incorporate the movements that will produce and keep your horse on the correct lead while maintaining his cadence and impulsion.

While it all may seem very complicated and confusing, sometimes the way to learn an idea or concept is to digest it piece by piece and then to reduce it to a simple formula that you find meaningful. In the case of riding a circle you might find the following chart helpful: Circle = Inside leg AT the girth, outside leg BEHIND the girth—which hardly says it all, but may prove to be just enough to bring the whole feeling to mind.

Halt

Ask just about anyone how to make a horse slow down or come to a halt, and nine times out of ten the answer will include a phrase such as "by pulling on the reins" or "by pulling him together," or something else that implies a tug-of-war with the horse. Although these ideas appear to make sense, they represent one of the most widespread misconceptions in the field of equitation. The fallacy of pulling a horse anywhere to do anything is readily apparent if you just take a moment to think about it. The average rider weighs anywhere from 110 to 175 pounds—the average horse weighs anywhere from 850 to 1200 pounds. Obviously there is little to be gained by instituting a pulling contest in which the odds are already stacked in the horse's favor.

One may very well ask, If you don't slow or stop a horse by pulling, then how DO you do it? The answer here is not necessarily the obvious, but ultimately is the only way. You cause a horse to slow down or come to a halt by *pushing* him forward into

Working on the circle. Inside leg AT the girth, outside leg BEHIND the girth.

the bit and, thereby, onto his hindquarters. To see how this works, imagine that you are mounted on a horse, walking toward a wall or fence. If you were to continue walking forward toward the fence without turning to the right or left, keeping your legs on the horse urging him forward, when you reached the fence you would have the sensation of pushing him into the fence and therefore to a halt (if only because he could not go any farther). This same sensation can be duplicated without the fence simply by squeezing the horse forward from your leg to your hand (which in this instance replaces the fence). If you hold him back with a steady pressure from your hands (not a "pull" but rather a "firm feel") and then by the pressure from your legs insist that the horse accept or move into the bit, you will find that he will halt neatly and squarely with his hindquarters well positioned.

We have now come to possibly the most important concept in all of riding. That is the idea that a horse cannot accomplish any move in any direction (including backing) unless he is prepared to move forward. What is so important about being prepared to move forward? A horse that is ready and able to move forward is one that has his hind legs placed so that he can literally spring in any direction at a moment's signal. By thus engaging his hindquarters he has accepted the responsibility of bearing the rider's weight and, most assuredly, is not looking for escape routes or resistances. Anytime that the rider feels that he is supporting more of the horse's weight with his hands than is comfortable, he immediately ought to apply a strong leg and seat to force the horse into self-carriage and to prevent him from leaning against the rider.

Although the idea of pushing a horse to a stop or from a faster gait to a slower one may seem peculiar at first, a few days of experimentation and practice should bring noticeable results. Begin by walking and halting, taking care to finish with all four feet squarely positioned and with a "light" feeling to your hands. If the horse is tipped onto his forehand, or if you just cannot seem to find him with your hands, then you have not succeeded in pushing him into your hands or into self-carriage. If you feel that he is too strong for you, then most likely he is being lazy with his hind end and allowing you to hold him up. This balkiness is just another way of saying that he has not engaged his hindquarters and that you must use your legs and seat twice as much to force him to hold himself together.

Bringing a horse to a halt by pushing him into the bit and onto his hindquarters.

Once you feel that you can halt neatly and easily from the walk, then try it from the sitting trot, posting trot, and canter. If at any time you become confused or cannot seem to effect a halt without a great deal of strain, then return to walking, or even to pushing your horse into a fence until you re-establish the idea of pushing. You might bear in mind that as the horse's rate of speed increases (such as from the walk to the canter), you must increase the amount of leg and seat which you use in order to push him to a halt.

Stated simply, the way to halt a horse is to sit deeper, squeeze the sides of your legs against the sides of the horse, slip your pelvis slightly forward, and hold your hands soft yet firm on the reins for the horse to move into. For a halt made from the walk or the canter you need only sit a little deeper to make the signal apparent to the horse. From a posting trot, however, the move must obviously be more definite in order for the horse to understand. The formula then, would be as follows: To halt: *Sit* down, *squeeze,* take a *deeper seat* and *hold back* on reins.

Half-Halt

The half-halt is a handy maneuver which can be interjected just about anywhere, anytime, and is used to collect the horse and make him bring his hocks (hindquarters) in underneath him. The half-halt simply consists of asking the horse to halt, having him respond *mentally* to your request, but then forcing him to move on before he can come to a complete stop. For example, you might be moving along at the posting trot, while your horse seems to be getting heavier and heavier in front. Instead of stopping to reorganize, you could sit down, squeeze your legs, use your seat, and support with your hands *as if you mean to halt.* At just the moment when your horse has gathered himself for the halt, with his hocks coming in underneath him and his forehand becoming decidedly lighter, squeeze your legs even stronger and soften your hands to allow him to continue forward at the trot. The overall effect would be one of simultaneously compressing and lightening your horse without a loss of forward motion.

To make a half-halt: think halt but move forward. This is a simple device that can be employed at any gait to lighten a horse that is lugging, to reorganize a horse that is too strung out, or even to divert an animal whose attention is wandering.

Transitions

One of the most beneficial exercises is that of transitions—transitions from the sitting trot to the posting trot or canter, from the canter to strong canter to halt, from the halt to the canter, and so on. Basically there are two types of transitions—from one gait to another (i.e., from the sitting trot to the canter to the walk) and within the same gait (i.e., ordinary canter to strong canter to very slow or collected canter). Regardless of the type of transition you are making, there is one rule that applies in every case: When the rider asks, transitions *must* be made promptly.

Transitions bring the horse's hocks underneath his body, thereby collecting him and improving his impulsion by the increased use of his hindquarters. Aside from being an excellent exercise, transitions also serve to keep a horse alert and interested in what is going to happen next. When making transitions it is particularly important to keep a feel of your horse's head. You do not want him to sprawl forward as you increase the pressure of your legs. For instance, if you were working at the sitting trot and wanted to lengthen your horse's stride, you would deepen your seat slightly. You could then employ your seat as well as your legs to urge your horse forward, increase the pressure of your legs against your horse's sides, and keep a soft yet firm feel of his mouth.

Essentially what you are requesting is that your horse open his stride—that is, cover more ground with each step, without increasing his speed. You are not asking him to canter or even to trot particularly fast but rather to lengthen his stride. In the beginning all you can expect is the correct execution of one, two, or possibly three steps before the horse becomes confused and tries to pick up speed or to break into another gait. To accentuate the difference for both horse and rider, it is always a good idea to return to the original gait after lengthening or shortening a stride. A little practice and patience—sitting trot to strong trot, sitting trot to canter, ordinary canter to strong canter, any one of these to halt, or any combination of these—will show surprising results in a relatively short period of time.

Although responding with the appropriate action takes precedence over everything, promptness is a vital part of the proper execution of a transition. Consequently, a response is not considered correct unless your signal has been answered immediately. The reason will become most apparent when you begin working at figures (such as eights or serpentines) or practicing on jumps. When jumping, in particular, there will be many instances in which you wish to move your horse up or take him back for the short stride in order to ride smoothly for a certain distance or turn. If your horse has become accustomed to answering your signals promptly with a lengthened or shortened stride, you will have no trouble adjusting to just about any situation. If, however, he delays for even so much as one stride, he may overshoot the line of your figure or land on his nose (and yours) in an obstacle.

Figure Eight

A figure eight is meant to be just that—two equal circles (one to the right and one to the left), both of which begin and end at a common point located at the exact center of the figure. When a figure eight is required as a test (as in a class at a horse show to determine the winner), it is usually to be performed first at the trot, demonstrating a change of diagonals, and then at the canter, demonstrating a change of leads—usually simple, but on occasion, flying. In more advanced classes, such as "open equitation," the judge may request that half the figure be performed at one gait, while the second half be performed at another. He may request, for example, that you trot the right hand circle sitting, trot the left hand circle posting, then canter the right hand circle and trot the left hand circle.

Since the starting point of your figure eight will influence the entire configuration, it is most important to plan ahead when you are choosing where to begin. You want to make sure that there is enough room in front, behind, and on either side of the spot to permit your circles to be round and identical in size. Remember that at least in the beginning you will need a lot of space. It is also helpful to select a spot that is somehow identifiable to you— such as one in line with a tree or bush, or in front of a certain jump or fence post. You will then have no problem returning to it each time you complete a circle.

Let us now assume that you have found a suitable starting point from which to work your eights. It is at the far end of the ring, exactly in the center, and in line with a large post. In the beginning you will want to use all the available space to insure that your circles really are round, and to give yourself enough time to plan your moves as you go along. A figure eight is just like everything else in riding; you must be able to make it work at the walk before you can expect to recognize the figure at the trot or canter. So take your time and walk it through once, twice, a dozen times.

On the first few attempts it might be helpful to count the actual number of steps in each circle in order to establish the pattern of uniformity and equality, which will later become a habit. For instance, from "X" (making the center point) walk six steps forward toward the marking post, then twelve steps to the right, then twelve steps toward the back, then twelve steps to the right again, and return to "X" with six more steps to the right, which heads you toward the post. Repeat the same pattern on the left hand to complete the figure of eight.

Once you become familiar with the pattern, you can turn your attention to finer points. With your horse bent in the direction in which he is heading, making the circles round should present no problem if you have done your "homework" in riding circles. Keeping the two sides equal should be just as easy, provided you have first walked it out in measured steps and have some idea of where you must go if both halves are to be the same. Precision and timing of your stops and starts will come with practice—lots of it.

At the trot you are expected to change your diagonal at a designated point—not before you get there and certainly not after you have crossed it. At the canter you are expected to make a simple change of lead that means come to a halt for a few seconds and then break off on the opposite lead. Of course, in order to accomplish a good figure eight, your horse must be alert, lively, and attentive to your signals. You, on the other hand, must be sensitive to his performance. You must pay particular attention to any tendency to chop off parts of the circle, anticipating the change of direction or gait in the center. If he takes off too quickly he may ruin the balance by proceeding in a straight line; if he hangs back, on the other hand, he may have to be driven forward to prevent him from falling out of the frame and thereby switching (unbidden) a slower gait.

Aside from the overall challenge of performing the "eight" correctly and uniformly, the most difficult part of the figure occurs at the canter when you must halt momentarily at "X" in order to carry out a simple change of lead. The most common mistake is overshooting or missing the center point; the ensuing maneuvers designed to bring the horse somewhere near "X" then compound the problem. This type of error is usually due to a lack of control and planning on the part of the rider. Since the rider knows that he wishes to halt at a particular point and change leads, it is up to him to share his secret with the horse and prepare him in advance for the stop. If he knows that his horse is hard to stop, he would be wise to keep his eight a little on the large side to allow a few extra strides for the halt. On the other hand, if his horse tends to hang back or is somewhat sluggish, chances are he will be doubly so when working on a circle. Particularly in the last quarter of the circle, a strong leg and seat will be required to keep him moving forward until he reaches "X." The horse must not be allowed to fall on his face at that point. He must not lose his impulsion (after which it would be difficult to get started again) nor just keep inching or lugging forward with tiny walking or jogging steps. All of the preceding indicate that the horse, not the rider, is actually in control.

Changes of Lead in a Straight Line

Another good exercise for both horse and rider is making simple changes of lead in a straight line. One can try this along a fence line, "down the center" of a ring, or in the middle of nowhere in particular. The hard part, of course, is keeping your horse working in a line without wandering from side to side or making a half-circle or tangent. In order to do this you will have to contain your horse within a chute comprised of your hands and legs so that he cannot stray to either the right or the left. Keep him moving forward from your leg to your hand, his mind definitely on the business at hand, and he will have neither the time nor the inclination to lose his way.

The horse must rely completely upon your signals to tell him which lead you want and when (he has no curve or bend to indicate which lead he ought to pick up). You must first be sure that both you and your horse are familiar with the same set of clues. Once the signals have been firmly established, this exercise can be both a test of discipline and an enjoyable challenge.

At first you would be wise to make your changes every eight or ten strides (yes, you must count strides), working several feet away from the ring fence or in your usual track around an unenclosed area. This spacing will give you plenty of time to think about each change and to prepare yourself and the horse accordingly. It does no good at all to get the correct leads if your horse has meandered, walked, and jogged as he pleased in between times. Precision and promptness are a part of the whole and must be given due consideration as you practice.

As you approach the last three or four strides before you wish to change your lead you can retrace the steps for halt (i.e., sit down, squeeze, take a deeper seat, and hold back on reins) and squarely bring your horse to a standstill on all four feet. Then hold him in that position for a few seconds; you can keep his attention by opening and closing your fingers lightly on the reins. At the same time shift your weight slightly onto the opposite hip, increase your leg pressure to ask for the lead you want, and use your usual hand signal along with a supporting feel from the other rein to keep him from turning or losing his line. In other words, canter a measured distance, halt, reorganize, and canter again on the opposite lead.

As you become more proficient at making changes you can decrease the number of strides between them until you are able to skip down a line changing leads every two or three strides. When you arrive at this level of performance, the halts are no longer genuine stops, but rather momentary hesitations in which the horse reorganizes his feet for the next lead.

Serpentine

A serpentine is another excellent exercise in discipline for both horse and rider. The configuration is simple enough—a series of parallel lines connected at the ends by half circles. The result is a figure comprised of a single line that hooks, snakelike, back and forth. Its execution, however, requires equal parts of patience and persistence. Great skill is needed to produce a uniform pattern in which the lines are truly parallel and straight, and joined by half circles that literally grow out of one line and melt into the next.

A serpentine may be worked in any area that is free of obstacles such as trees or jumps in all directions (although it is customary when working in a ring to work the figure across its width). Allow room for three or more crosses and turns. Again, it would be wise to walk the pattern first in order to acquaint your horse with your wishes and to plan exactly where you want to go and how you will make your turns.

It may be helpful, initially, to have some kind of guide to follow. Therefore, imagine a line that runs down the center of the serpentine, dividing the figure into right-handed and left-handed loops. Either visualize or mark it on the ground you are working on; pretend, furthermore, that there are a series of posts placed on the line at equal distances from each other. Perform the serpentine along this guideline, turning to alternate sides to avoid make-believe obstacles.

Begin the configuration by riding in a straight line to the starting point. Circle to your right until you cross the imaginary centerline. Rather than continuing in the same direction, having made a half circle to your right, turn to do a half circle to your left. Follow the second half circle with a third, this time to the right again. Alternating direction as you move from one side of the guideline to the other, continue your turns until you have completed the number that you planned or that space allows. At this time, you may either halt squarely and stand for five or ten seconds, or you may complete the second half of the last circle to continue the serpentine in reverse, then return to your original starting point, halt, and stand to finish. Whichever you choose, the diameters of all the half circles should be equal, the maximum of each curve should be the same distance from the guideline, and the segments that cross the line should all be parallel.

The posting trot and the canter require a change in diagonal or lead with every change in direction of the serpentine. The change should be made as you cross the center, so that you are prepared for the turn before you reach the curve. If you were finishing a half circle to the left, appropriately riding on the left diagonal or lead, you would switch to the right as you cross the guideline, in anticipation of the approaching right turn. Finishing that half circle, you would change again to the left.

Half of each cross is ridden on one diagonal or lead and the other half is ridden on the opposite diagonal or lead, taking care to be on the correct one as you ride *into* the turns.

The straightness of your lines and the roundness of your half circles will depend largely upon how well you use your legs to instruct your horse in what is expected of him, to detect (not anticipate!) any actual deviations, and to make any corrections which may be needed. The overall skill with which you perform the serpentine will depend upon just how adept you are at trotting and cantering both straight lines and circles as well as how you handle the necessary changes of diagonals and leads. In fact, one of the nice things about a serpentine is that it gives you an opportunity to put these things together to form a definite configuration.

UNPROGRAMMED RIDES

This is the "free thought" riding which can brighten any practice session. Instead of just riding around with only an occasional change of direction or configuration, you might try riding freely for five, ten, or fifteen minutes, letting each movement flow naturally. The first and only requirement is that there be no definite direction or gait in which you are to work. The more varied and imaginative your ride, the more fun it will be for both you and your horse. Consider yourself and the horse as a unit. The general idea is to keep your mind a little more than one jump ahead of the unit. For example, if you were working in a ring you might begin with a sitting trot around the perimeter one complete time. If your thoughts need a little push to get in motion, you might leave the rail at some point to trace a letter "M" at a posting trot. (Letters and numerals, by the way, are great starters.) This could be followed by a half-halt and a half circle at a canter on whichever lead happens to suit you, then a complete halt and canter off on the other lead across the ring on a diagonal line. Upon reaching the rail you could make a transition to a sitting trot, turn a line down the center, and work a few serpentine crosses at the strong trot. Come back to a slow trot on the ends, drift into a posting trot for a stride or two and then into a canter for a couple of changes of lead in a straight line. Anything goes, and the only thing you have to watch for is a tendency to become so absorbed in creating your own program that you allow yourself to get sloppy in your riding or to accept a lesser degree of performance from the horse.

While this type of riding can be a combination brain teaser and treat, it also provides the additional features of improving the co-ordination of the horse and rider as a team, making the horse more supple, and offering a pleasant diversion within the daily routine—one in which the animal is forced to listen to and for his rider's signals, since there is no prescribed route for him to follow or anticipate.

When you are able to dream up patterns and programs as you go—using the walk, trot, and canter, changes of lead and diagonals, as well as simple transitions—and are capable of performing them with a fair amount of control and precision, you have obviously reached at least a basic level of proficiency. Otherwise you would not be able to channel your mind and your body in two directions at once and control the horse as well.

Jumps

As soon as you feel at ease with the gaits and can use them comfortably to execute simple maneuvers, you are ready to extend your horizon to jumping. This is not to imply that at some earlier stage in your learning process you could not have managed to stay on while your horse jumped one or more obstacles. However, a haphazard introduction to jumping before a rider has established his position on the flat and gained a minimal amount of confidence frequently leads to abominable habits that are detrimental to the rider's form and most discouraging to the horse. For example, the rider who manages to hang on over a fence by balancing his weight against the horse's mouth is laying the perfect foundation for a pair of rough and heavy hands. This will be difficult to correct. He would be much better off to wait to try jumping until his legs can support his body, his hands free to follow the horse's head and neck as he uses them in his arc.

Another and possibly stronger reason for establishing a good basis of flat work before attempting to jump is that a jump is the logical and inevitable conclusion of the events leading up to the take-off. In order to effect a good jump the rider must have the ability to see and place his horse somewhere within the striking

94

zone—the area from which the animal can negotiate the fence without strain—while maintaining the right cadence, impulsion, and balance. To accomplish this, it is important that the rider be in a position that enables him to influence his horse before the jump. A rider who is frozen in a jumping position ten strides in front of a fence with his body already committed to the horse's flight is in for a rude awakening (and a short trip to the ground) should the animal suddenly decide to deviate from a straight line and steady rhythm toward and over the fence—run past the fence or dig in with his toes and refuse. On the other hand, a rider who is well positioned in his half-seat, with his weight evenly distributed and over his lower leg, can effectively deal with almost any situation. Because his legs are supporting his body, his hands are free to direct and follow the horse's movement. With his weight evenly distributed over a solid base and his upper body in balance, he is able to use his legs to keep his horse moving forward in a straight line and to maintain impulsion. Furthermore, when the horse reaches the point of take-off, all the rider will have to do is close his hip angle slightly as he drops his weight even more onto his knees and into his heels; he should then move his hands forward along the horse's crest to allow the animal full use of his head and neck when he leaves the ground. He could not be as free and easy with his body were he not in balance with both himself and his horse; and he could not be as secure in his position had he not first spent the time and expended the effort to build his muscles and confidence on the flat.

You are ready for jumping when you have done your homework on the flat. You should then be relatively secure in the half-seat, able to maintain your position while making circles as well as lines, and able to squeeze a sulky horse forward with your legs without landing with a thud.

AT THE TROT

The best advice that anyone can offer the beginning jumping rider is to *wait! Wait* on the approach—the fence will still be there. *Wait* for the take-off—you might be able to make the horse leave out a stride by leaping out of the saddle onto his neck, but that will just confuse him. *Wait* to land—once the horse leaves the ground he won't land any quicker if you unfold like a jack-in-the-box, drop on his back, cause him to hang a leg, and get tangled in the fence. The best method is simply to get into your half-seat and wait for the fence to happen. When the horse takes off, you sink down around him as he comes up underneath you. Keep your body still, but follow with your hands as he rounds his back and extends his neck in flight. Return to your original position as he reaches out to land—first with your body and then with your hands. The complete operation requires less than 20 degrees of movement with your upper body and only as much motion with your hands as is necessary to follow the horse's head without abandoning him. If you think about your half-seat in terms of your hip angle, it ought to be at 65 or 70 degrees on the approach. When your horse leaves the ground you should close that angle slightly to about 50 degrees. Leaning or ducking forward looks bad and exposes you to being hit in the face, shoulders, or chest as the horse rises to meet you.

Cross Rail

The cross rail is an ideal beginning fence because it is easily adjusted to varying minimal heights by simply widening or closing the space between the standards, and because the center cross provides a focal point for both horse and rider.

A worthwhile starting exercise is trotting in your half-seat over eighteen-inch-high cross rails that have been positioned around the outer edge of the ring along the fence. It is wise either to equip the jumps with wings on both sides or place the jumps close enough to the ring fence to prevent the horse from ducking out on that side. On the other side, run a rail from the top of the standard to the ground. This eliminates the need for any great amount of steering on the rider's part, leaving him free to concentrate on his position and to get the feel of jumping.

At this point, you cannot expect to assume and maintain even a mediocre position over the fence. Just try to keep your weight evenly distributed and your legs as quiet as possible throughout. Concentrate on maintaining contact with your thigh and lower leg and start the move with your hands early enough so that you do not catch the horse in the mouth as he jumps. Close your hip angle slightly with the impulsion of the horse as he takes off, and return

"Ducking," a common fault of riders while jumping, has the rider jumping up on the horse's neck. Not only does this look bad, but "ducking" forward exposes the rider to being hit in the face, shoulders, or chest as the horse rises to meet you.

to your before-take-off position as the horse starts to land. It is not easy at first to maintain any position, much less a correct one, while jumping. You are apt to find that you are first too far behind and then suddenly too far ahead of the horse's motion, so quickly that both seem to happen at the same time. You may feel that you ought to be doing more or that you are doing too much, or that the horse is going too fast or too slow, or, most frequently, that you are out of balance and are about to be snapped off the back end or off one side or another. One of the hardest things to learn is not to look directly at the fence you are jumping, but to look ahead at a fixed point beyond. "Heads up, heels down" is as applicable to jumping as it is to the flat.

In the beginning one fence on either side of the ring is enough. While this may seem overcautious or tame, there is enough to think about at first to make most people grateful for the chance to get organized between fences. When you have gained sufficient confidence working over two fences, you are ready to increase the number of jumps. Take care to leave enough room between fences to permit time to think and organize. If the area is small and there is room for only one or two fences, increase the number of rounds instead. Whichever way you do it, add jumps until you can handle at least eight consecutively. Thus, you will get your first taste of steering your horse between fences as well as jumping more than one at a time.

The average horse's stride is considered to be twelve feet. To make the striding work out between fences, the fences should be placed at distances that are multiples of twelve feet. Allowing six feet each for take-off and landing, twenty-four feet equals one stride, thirty-six feet equals two, and forty-eight equals three. The twelve-foot-stride measurement will be particularly important later, when calculating the placement of cantering fences—especially for combinations of two to four fences. These combinations are designed to be jumped in sequence with either one, two, or three strides between them.

Fences spaced at the multiples of twelve-foot distances generally ride easily and on stride. Being aware of a measured distance between fences can be a great help in preparing to ride through it. An awareness of the distance enables you to know ahead of time just how many strides to expect between a given pair of fences. Unfortunately, there are variations. If one of the fences is peculiar looking or strange to the horse, he may hesitate or shorten his stride just enough to require an extra stride, or he might overgauge the first fence and take one less stride to the second. Should your fences be situated on a hill or grade, furthermore, both you and your horse would soon find that jumping uphill is longer than jumping downhill.

You cannot spend enough time practicing trotting fences. In the very beginning you should just get in your half-seat and stay there throughout the approach, make a slight move forward as the horse leaves the ground, and return to your half-seat immediately upon landing. As you improve, you can modify your approach somewhat and use a sitting trot until the last two or three strides, at which time you should assume a half-seat.

You should never attempt to ride to a fence from a posting trot. It is very difficult to time things so that you are out of the saddle when the horse takes off; should you be so unfortunate as to be sitting down at that moment, you are apt to find yourself neatly catapulted onto the horse's neck.

Although you are sitting down on the approach at a sitting trot, the intent is to get into a half-seat prepared to move forward. Sitting down as a result of posting is part of a two-position movement, the next part of which should be up, not forward and over the fence. It is decidedly harder, therefore, to get with the horse if you approach the jump from the posting-trot position. Furthermore, it is much easier to feel and correct potential problems during the approach from a sitting trot than from a posting trot.

Straight Rails

When you begin to feel at home trotting cross rails, it is time to move on to straight rails. For starters, you would be wise to return to one fence approximately two feet high on either side of the ring. Since you will not have the center-point illusion of the cross rail as a guide, place a rail on the ground between the standards at the base of the fence as a ground line to guide both you and your horse.

Here again, you will be glad to have the chance to reorganize yourself after each fence. As the fences become higher, the tendency of the horse to land cantering increases. Since you do not want to canter just yet, you will need plenty of time to regain your trot before reaching the next obstacle. Follow the same procedure you had with the placement of cross rails, but increase the number of fences and raise the height until you can negotiate eight or twelve consecutive fences measuring two and one-half to three feet in height. During this time what you are actually doing is familiarizing yourself with the look and feel of riding down to and over a jump.

Spread and Square Fences

Up until now we have been dealing with single fences composed of one or more elements in the same vertical plane—that is, one or more rails placed on top of one another on the same pair of standards. Trotting to such fences poses no particular problem and requires no specialized approach. When jumping these vertical fences, neither the flight of the horse from take-off to landing nor the resulting feel to the rider lasts very long. They are, therefore, relatively hard to discern. In order to exaggerate the feel and prolong the actual flight time, let's introduce ourselves to one of the most useful tools available, the spread fence—and, more specifically, the square oxer or square fence.

A square fence consists of one or more elements in the same horizontal plane—that is, a spread fence whose components are parallel and separated by at least two or more feet. In the beginning you may want to try a square fence spread only eighteen inches, although in order to be truly square it ought to be as wide as it is high—i.e., three feet high by three feet wide. The common practice is to make it even wider than it is high. Naturally a horse jumping a square fence spends more time in the air than when jumping a single rail, so the feeling of flight is intensified. In addition, a horse jumping a square fence uses his body more as he rounds his back and stretches his neck to clear the second element. This provides a more pronounced "feel" of jumping and an excellent opportunity to follow his motion with your hands.

Placement Fence

As soon as you are presented with a spread fence of any sort, you are immediately faced with the problem of a more definitive take-off area as well as the need for more refinement in the approach. If the horse should "stand away" (leave the ground from a point too far in front of the fence), he might meet his arc before he meets the fence and thus crash into the last element as he lands. To avoid the latter and still be able to practice with square and spread fences, now is the time to acquaint yourself with a basic form of equine gymnastics—the placement fence. As the name implies, this is a fence that is put in front of another so that when the horse jumps it, he is automatically placed in the correct position for jumping the second fence. This removes any need on the part of the rider to see the distance and place his horse accordingly, or to wonder how many strides his horse will take before jumping a specific fence. Since the placement fence literally takes the guesswork out of jumping and can be constructed at anytime, anywhere, it is the perfect schooling instrument for both horse and rider.

An eighteen-inch cross rail, placed fifteen to eighteen feet in front of a two- to two-and-one-half-foot square oxer makes a fine start. With this distance, on a trotting approach the horse will barely hop over the cross rail, take one normal cantering stride, and jump out over the square fence. Wings are again in order to minimize the alternatives open to the horse and to allow the rider freedom to concentrate on maintaining his position and "feel" throughout both jumps.

Riding to a gymnastic differs slightly from riding to a single fence in that your horse must be a little more lively in order to negotiate two fences in a row. There are two parts to the gymnastic and only one stride between them, so there is very little time for the rider to prepare himself for the second obstacle. For this reason the rider usually finds it best to maintain his jumping position from take-off at the placement fence to landing after the second fence. He thereby eliminates the possibility of being left behind while going over the second. It is not unusual for the beginning jumping rider to be decidedly behind the horse's motion (despite what appears to be more than ample preparedness) when encountering his first spread fences. The way in which a horse extends himself and uses his body causes the time gap. The wider the spread, the more pronounced the feeling of overall extension as the horse reaches for the last element.

Because the sensation of jumping is more pronounced when a horse uses himself over a spread, there is that much more chance for the rider to lose his balance to either side, to be left at the take-off, or to be snapped back in midflight. In order to counteract the threat to his balance, the rider is forced to stay as close as possible to the horse's center of gravity. To accomplish this, stay well over the middle of the saddle (as opposed to leaning too far forward or remaining too vertical), push as much weight as possible through your knees and into your heels, keep your body as quiet as possible, and allow the *horse* to do the jumping.

This brings us to one of the most important concepts related to the act of riding horses over fences—let the horse do the jumping! It is a widespread fallacy among a large number of riders that many, many gyrations and contortions climaxed by one tremendous leap out of the saddle onto the withers, neck, or ears of the horse are necessary to get to the other side.

In reality the opposite is true. The less commotion caused by the rider, the smoother and steadier the jump is likely to be. It is thus easier for the rider to maintain his balance and position. Unnecessary yanking, kicking, elbow flapping, and body motion serve only to confuse and distract the horse from the next obstacle. The rider has a much better chance of creating and maintaining the proper amount of impulsion by the subtle yet firm use of his legs; kicking and flapping can only divert the horse's attention from the forward signals being issued.

The unexplainable leap out of the saddle as the horse leaves the ground serves no purpose and actually causes several problems which otherwise would not exist. The "chip in and get left" syndrome is a classic. As the rider propels himself out of the saddle and onto the horse's neck, the momentum carrying him forward is greatly increased by the thrust created by the horse leaving the ground. It then becomes nearly impossible for the rider to keep his legs under him—which further compounds his problems. Now he is no longer in a position from which he can control the outcome or the immediate aftermath of the jump. By springing up at the horse, the rider has totally committed his own body to the completion of the jump. However, if he has made a small miscalculation with regard to distance or has been slightly off in his timing, the rider is quite apt to find himself lying out on the neck of a horse who should and will take another stride before leaving the ground. In such a situation the results are most predictable. The horse stabs in a shortened stride (often raising his head abruptly as he does so) which has the effect of snapping the rider back into the saddle; the motion resembles a whiplash. The rider is then completely unprepared for the jump, which is just beginning. The horse takes off, literally jumping out from under the rider who, for the second time in a matter of seconds, is pushed even farther behind the motion. At this point the rider is apt to have considerable trouble even staying in the middle of the horse and frequently gropes around for anything with which to steady himself. All too often the nearest "anything" is the reins and, thus, the horse's mouth. (Actually, under such circumstances or in any "left" situation, the rider ought to allow the reins to slip through his fingers and grab a handful of mane or the horse's neck while attempting to regain his balance.) If the horse and rider somehow manage to arrive on the landing side of the fence as a single unit, several strides will be necessary before the rider can organize his reins, seat, and legs to some semblance of order and once again establish command of the horse.

An extra stride is not the only consequence of "jumping up" in front of a fence. On the contrary, the rider can get just as left if his move precipitates the take-off, thus causing the horse to leave out a stride he ought to have taken. In this case the rider makes his move a little early, usually in an effort to be prepared for the push-off by being there ahead of time. Instead, he is suddenly airborne. The horse has been confused into leaving the ground prematurely. Caught off guard, he frequently forgets to fold his legs properly (known as hanging a leg), twists his hindquarters, or tries in some other way to compensate for having been surprised into jumping. The rider, who had expected his horse to take another stride, is as unprepared for flight this time as he was for the extra stride previously. He is flipped back into the saddle and onto the horse's mouth. Here again, upon landing, he must rearrange himself completely in order to transmit even the simplest message to his horse.

AT THE CANTER

Let's assume that you recognize the possible complications arising from getting ahead of your horse in front of a fence and are able to overcome any such tendencies. Does this mean that you

A classic example of getting "left."

are assured of a trouble-free jumping career? Not exactly. What, then, are some of the problems that might crop up to impede your progress, and what can you do to avoid or rectify them?

So far we have only discussed trotting to fences, and while a great amount of groundwork can be laid and confidence built in this manner, sooner or later the time will come when you must begin cantering. The transition is not difficult to make mainly because the feel of an average jump is easily likened to the higher, longer cantering stride. Aside from everything happening a little faster so that there is less time to think and organize, most people find it a lot easier to canter to fences than to trot. Any easy introduction to cantering fences is effected by *trotting to the first of two fences* that have been placed three or four strides apart, and then allowing the horse to *land cantering and to go on to the next fence*. Since the distance is measured the rider can simply count strides and be completely confident that things will "work out" — much like riding through a simple gymnastic. After a while you can canter to the first fence as well, and from this point on you will need to know the meaning of timing and the importance of learning to see a distance.

As with the trotting fences, the cantering approach at this level should be ridden in a half-seat. If you are working with the prospect of showing in mind, then this is a good time to practice making a nice, round circle before proceeding to the first fence. Start your circle at the trot and then break into a canter when you are about halfway around.

Once you have completed your circle and are cantering in a straight line toward the jump, you will realize that the number of strides between you and the fence is completely variable and dependent upon the size of each individual stride. You will probably find it more difficult to judge the distance and timing of the cantered jump because of this. Once you have mastered it, however, you will undoubtedly appreciate the greater freedom that flexibility brings and will adjust your horse's stride so that he arrives at the fence in the proper position for the take-off without being forced to reach to shorten at the last minute. It is practically impossible to develop skill in timing without learning to see the distance, and both are essential to a smooth performance over fences. Timing is the ability to find just the right spot from which to take off, making the necessary adjustments before the final strides. Seeing a distance involves determining the length of your horse's stride in a proper ratio to the decreasing distance from the fence, and executing the adjustments in his stride as the need arises.

Obviously you cannot hope to achieve any sort of continuity over a course if you have no idea of where you are in relation to a given fence or if each time the horse leaves the ground it comes as a complete surprise to you. Consequently it is most important that you begin to look for the distance to your fences as soon as you are able to approach a jump with any degree of confidence. Watching other people ride over fences and counting the number of strides they get with different types of movers is an excellent way to familiarize yourself with timing. Four or five strides before they reach the jump decide whether or not they will have to make an adjustment and, if so, what sort it ought to be. Even better, of course, is doing it yourself. If you do not want to jump a zillion fences while developing an eye for distance, you can get the general idea by riding past actual jumps or rails placed on the ground. Announce to yourself or to a friend who's willing to listen whether you think you will get there long, short, or on stride. From the beginning, see how many times you call it correctly and how your average improves with practice. Ultimately you can expand this exercise to include actually making the adjustments you think necessary, but at the outset you simply want to test your own concept of distance.

It will not take long for you to discover that the more fences you jump, the easier it gets. This is mainly because as your confidence grows, your tension diminishes, an occurrence readily transmitted to the horse. In addition, the more relaxed you become the greater the likelihood of your being able to sit your horse instead of perch atop him. Riding easy, or relaxed, is a great help when you are jumping. In the first place, it will increase your ability to absorb the shock involved in take-off and landing. In the second, if you are relaxed when you find yourself caught in a difficult situation (such as being badly left) you will be able to handle it by disregarding form, simply folding up your body and dropping your weight into your heels so as to be carried safely over the fence. A tense or apprehensive rider caught in the same set of circumstances stands a good chance of being jumped off, thrown off balance, or planted in the middle of a fence.

A well-planned fence results in a fluid, pleasing picture of both horse and rider.

EXERCISES

There are almost as many exercises and theories for improving your jumping as there are riders, but here are a few with which to start.

1. Trot in a half-seat to a gymnastic which is eighteen inches to two feet at the "in" and two to three feet at the "out" (this can be a vertical in the beginning and later made square). Move your hands out to the side away from the horse's neck as he takes off for the first fence and be sure that your reins are sufficiently long so they do not catch him in the mouth. Do not put them back until he has landed over the second fence. This forces your weight into your heels and assures that your leg, not your hand, is supporting your body. It can also be worked at the canter, but the distance should then be widened between the fences to twenty-two or twenty-four feet.

2. Ride through gymnastics consisting of four or more fences with varied distances between each jump pair. All distances should ride easily in one, two, or three strides and the fences should be both spreads and verticals. The idea here is to improve your balance and your ability to follow the horse's motion by riding through a series of different jumps in which everything has already been measured and should therefore work out on-stride and smooth.

3. Jump a simple gymnastic or single fence on a circle, that is, turn either to the right or to the left after each fence and then return to the middle of that fence as a part of your continuing circle. You should alternate sides, turning first to one side and then to the other. The constant turning gives you something else to think about besides the jump, as well as improving your ability to land and turn or leave the ground while riding out of a turn. The tighter your turns the harder it is to get right to the fence and the sharper you have to be in both thinking and coordination. After a while you will learn to turn your horse in the air by shifting your weight and employing a subtle signal with hand, leg, or both.

4. Jump without stirrups. This should not be attempted until you are fairly confident with stirrups and feel that dropping your

irons will not result in your hanging onto your horse's mouth for balance. Once you can handle it, there is no exercise comparable to jumping without stirrups to improve your overall balance and strengthen your legs.

5. If you feel that you are riding too far ahead of your horse or anticipating the jumps, try the following. Have someone stand near a single fence with a fairly long approach. Trot toward the fence with the intention of allowing the other person to decide whether you will or will not jump. If he wants you to jump, he should remain silent. If he does not want you to jump, he should call out "halt!" In either case, he should not say anything until you are two or three strides at the most away from the fence. Since you have no way of knowing what he will say, you cannot commit yourself either to jumping or stopping until the last minute. Because it is definitely harder to halt a willing horse in front of a fence than it is to get with that jump, your tendency will be to ride prepared for the possibility of a halt. This in itself is enough to keep you in the middle of your horse and to discourage an inclination to anticipate the jump. As you become more familiar with this particular exercise you can increase the height of the fence, work both at the trot and the canter, and tell the caller not to speak until the last stride. Using your seat and weight as much as you can, you must, of course, take care to halt your horse properly. Be sure to praise him when he halts so he understands that you really did not want him to jump that time. Many consecutive or rough stops are not in order, for the horse may well become confused and think he should halt instead of jump fences in general. Despite the hazard of overly rough halts or possible confusion for the horse, this remains one of the best exercises for learning to "wait for the fence to happen."

6. Since the best and only approach to a certain fence may not always be a straight line to the center, if only to find out what it feels like you ought to try jumping a few fences at an angle. The fences need not be high, and trotting is in order at the start. You then have a good chance of placing your horse exactly where you want him. If you approach the jump from the extreme right-hand side and plan to reach it somewhere slightly to the left of

A well-balanced fence for both horse and rider.

center, remember that as you leave the ground you should treat it as a jump either on a right-hand circle or a straight forward. This will enable you to find the right spot as well as enough room to jump; whereas if you tried to ride a straight line on the diagonal you would ultimately pass the possible take-off points and run out to the left past the fence. Trotting lazy eights (figure eights done on their sides, western style) across a single fence is a perfect way to teach your eye to compensate for the optical illusions created by an angled approach.

Ultimately you can make up jumping courses for yourself. Begin with simple fences, evenly spaced and in line with each other, and graduate to more complicated ones that include difficult turns, combinations, and jumping across fences on an angle.

As you work on your riding and jumping, try to remember that at best you are dealing with a factor of unpredictability—the horse. Bear in mind that he is not the brightest creature in the animal kingdom and that he does not always understand what is expected of him despite the first, tenth, or twentieth request. Realize that you may make unreasonable demands without meaning to and that the lines of communication between you and your horse are not always clear. Understand that the art of riding is a continuous learning process requiring practice and patience, and that loss of skill and coordination are the usual prices paid for lapses in application. Control your temper as best you can and remind yourself that the instant you feel anger toward the horse, you have ceased striving for unity in your performance and have begun striving for only yourself. Accept the fact that not everyone is mentally and/or physically equipped to be an outstanding rider, but remember that inadequacies can frequently be more than amply compensated for (as in the case of an overly timid rider with a fantastic set of hands). Be satisfied with small signs of progress over long periods of time —suddenly feeling "right" in your half-seat or free to put your hands on your head over a fence when previously it would have meant a quick trip to the ground. Above all, know that there is no end to what you can learn about horses and riding. What is applicable to one horse is quite apt to be meaningless to the next; what worked today may fail tomorrow. Every person who has ever ridden seriously has a favorite trick or a "would you believe" story to relate, and there is something to be gained from each and every one.

Index